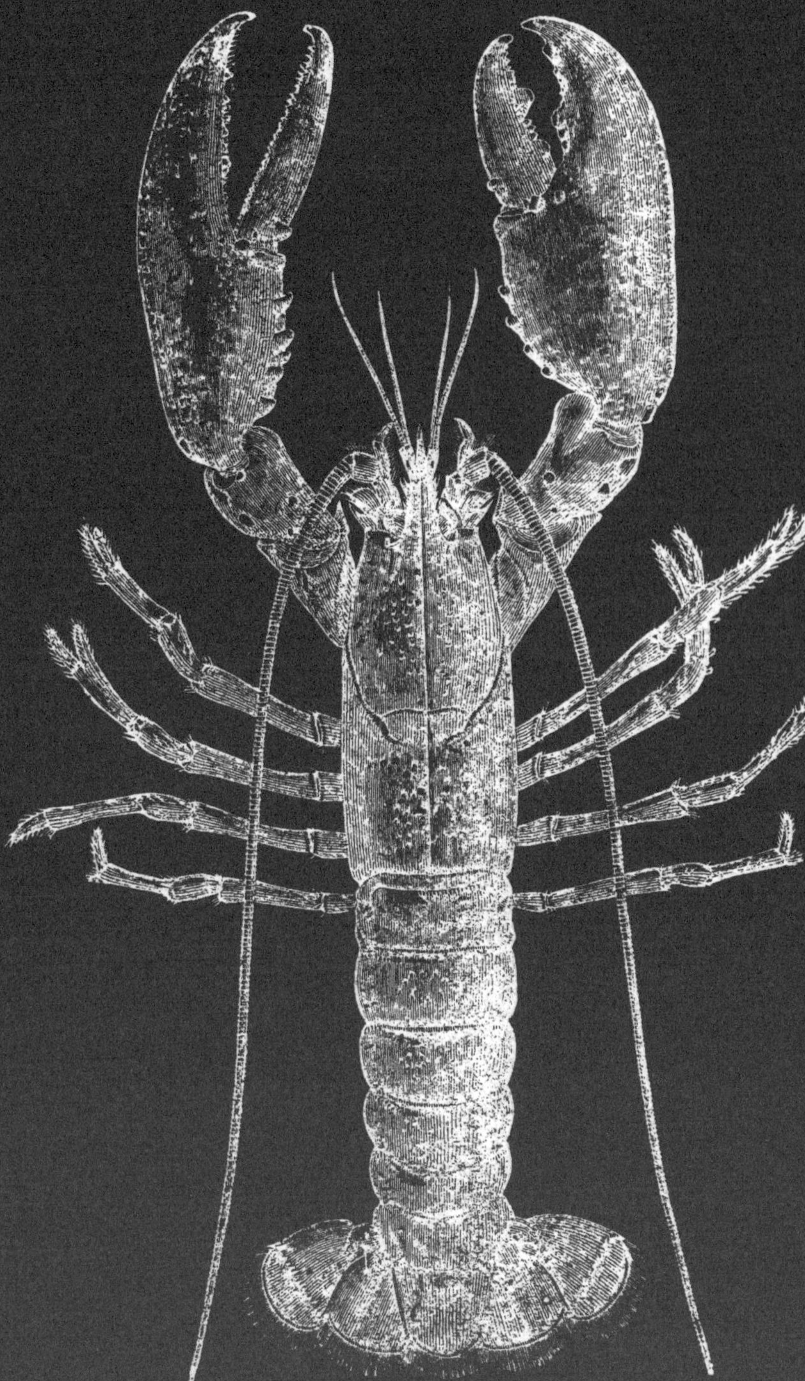

THE LOBSTER'S TALE

CHRIS PRICE

and

BRUCE FOSTER

MASSEY UNIVERSITY PRESS

What is the lobster's tune when he is boiled?

Thomas Lovell Beddoes

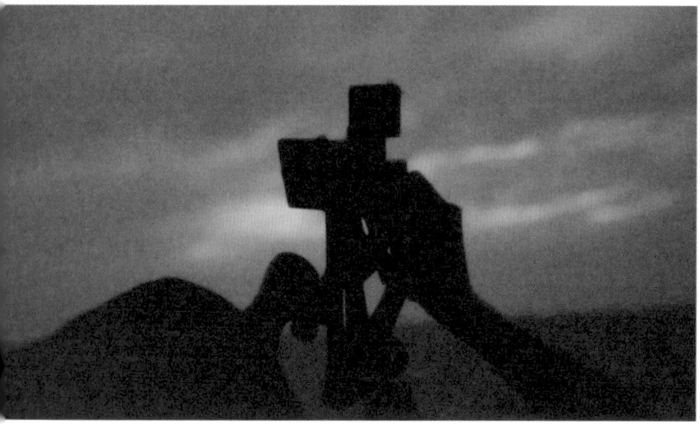
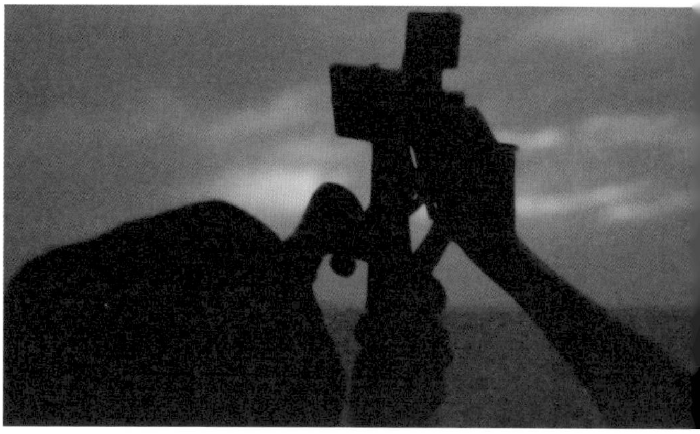

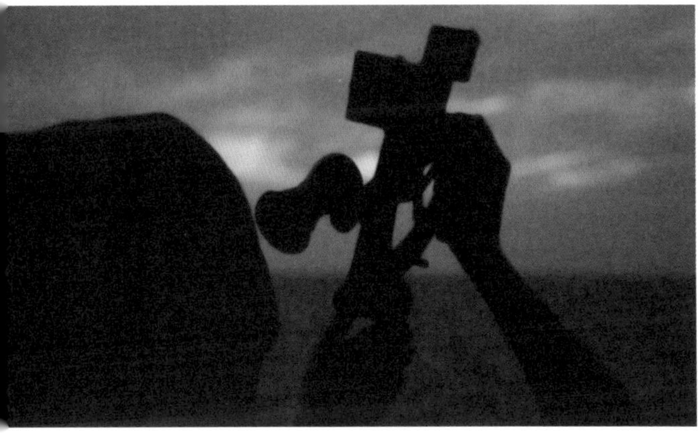

Although its etymology stretches back to the Old English *loppestre*, and beyond that to a corruption of the Latin *locusta*, both the form and the meaning of the word 'lobster' have remained remarkably steady throughout the centuries. Some words that have lived in the world for a similar length of time have spread and branched, occupying new habitats and discarding old. Look at the many uses of the word 'husk' if you want an example. The lobster, however, has remained the lobster, a singular term for a singular creature.

Asked to consider the lobster, many people might turn to gastronomy: thermidor, bisque, *homard à l'Américaine*. But the lobster I first think of is Thibault.

~

. . . One day I realise that

Thibault was a blue-black Breton lobster of the species *Homarus gammarus*. He was also a blue-blooded creature — the presence of copper in his blood made it so — and when he walked under the shady trees of the elegantly manicured Jardin du Palais-Royal, located just behind the Comédie-Française, he wore a blue silk ribbon. Rescued from the nets of La Rochelle, he had arrived in Paris as the domestic companion of a young translator and poet, member of a coterie of writers who would come to be known as the Petit Cénacle. Defending his choice of Thibault over the more usual pets, Gérard de Nerval asked, 'Why should a lobster be any more ridiculous than a dog? Or a cat, or a gazelle, or a lion, or any other animal that one chooses to take for a walk?'

He singled out their quiet, unobtrusive qualities. 'I have a liking for lobsters. They are peaceful, serious creatures. They know the secrets of the sea, they don't bark, and they don't gnaw upon one's *monadic* privacy like dogs do. And Goethe had an aversion to dogs, and he wasn't mad.' Dogs, today, are *interdit* in the Jardin du Palais-Royal.

~

like the diving bell spider I can take my bubble with me and go walking in the world below the

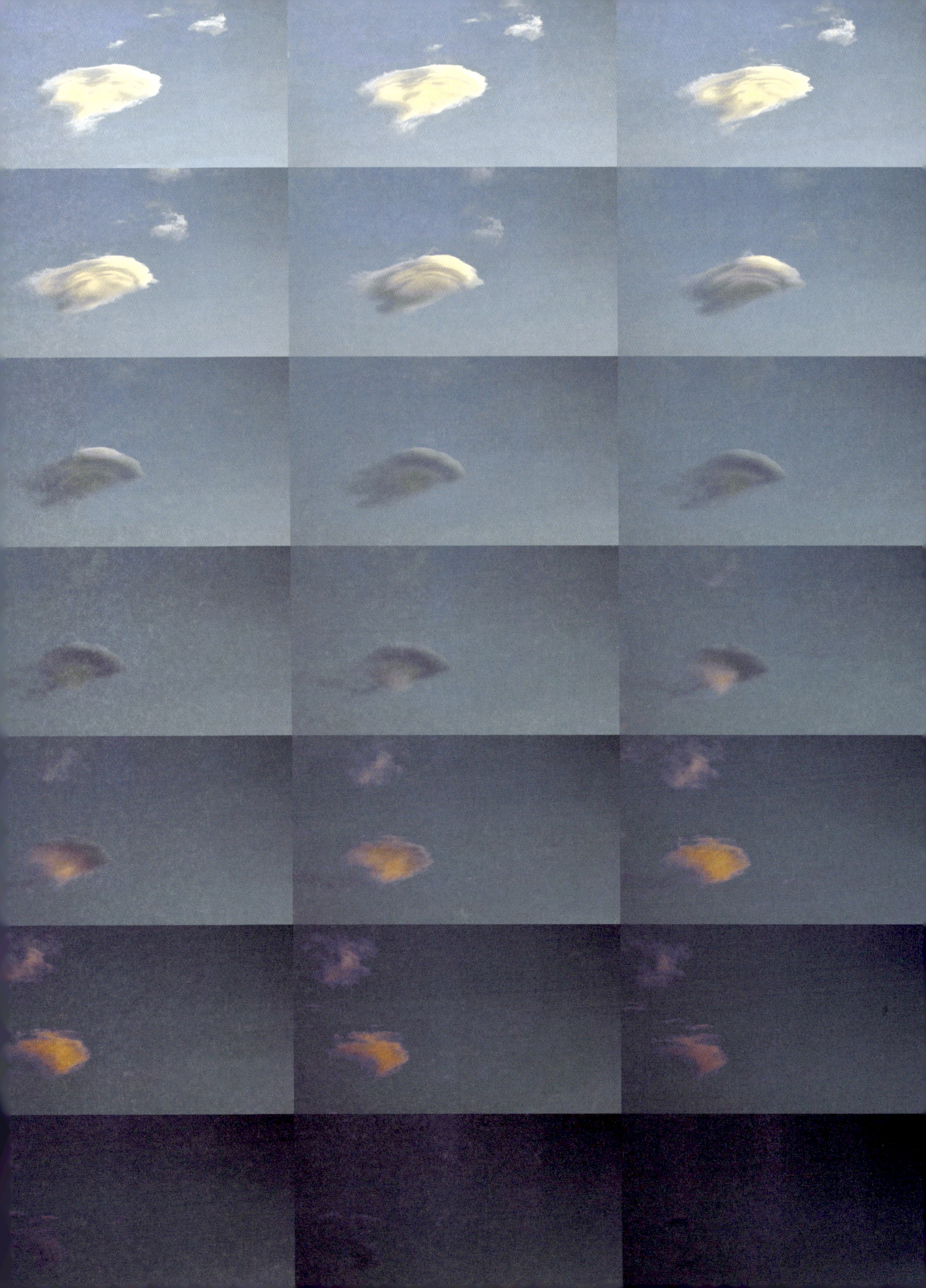

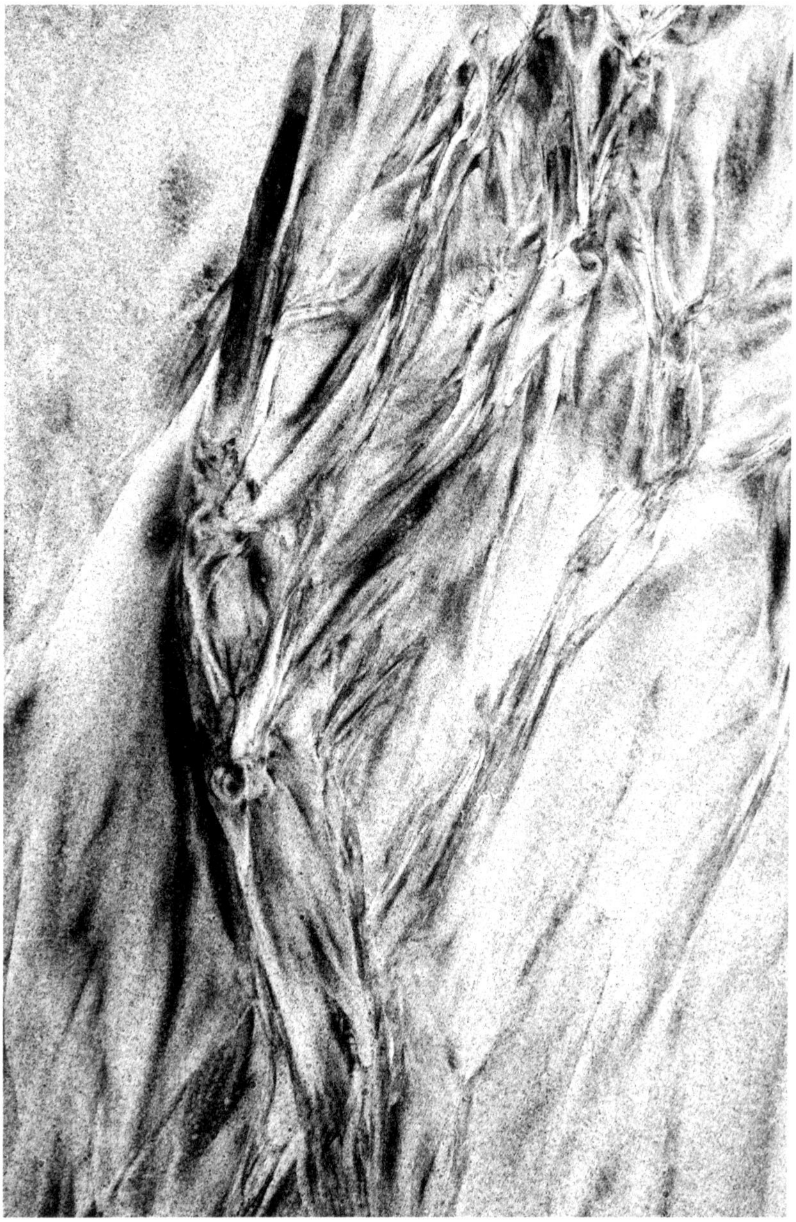

waterline. Water has many mouths, and as I sink below the surface of what I want to say, bubbles

As zoologists know and poets may be only half aware, 'the lobster' is not an undivided entity. Under the carapace of that single word lies a branching Linnaean order. When David Foster Wallace considered the pain of the lobster in the title essay of his 2005 collection, he focused on *Homarus americanus*, another of the clawed lobsters that are the prototype for our cartoon images of creatures with eyes on stalks and outsized pincers.
In England, Nerval is known primarily for his lobster, whereas in France the lobster has not occupied such a dominant position in the author's mythology. On that side of the Channel, Thibault hides in a crevice, while in England he strolls about in plain view, almost obscuring his owner. As Wallace remarks, 'there's much more to know than most of us care about'.

~

rise from secret openings, air within meniscus, water balloons built to self-destruct. Let the messages

Some lobsters are nomadic, others migrate. Migrants adopt the methods by which the West was won. Walking or running across the open seafloor, and hence vulnerable to attack, they follow the leader in a long train, each lobster using its antennae to maintain contact with the one in front. The formation reduces drag and therefore requires less collective effort. The final lobster is the train's rear guard, delegated to do battle with any predator that might attack from behind. When threatened as a group, the lobsters circle their wagon-shells and turn outwards to defend themselves.

~

An English churchman who became a soldier was said to have 'boiled his lobster', changing colour from clerical blue to redcoat. Lobster-tail armour, used in the eighteenth century, was a flexible construction of overlapping metal plates. Rather than encasing the soldier in a rigid canister, it moved with the occupant. The lobster itself is even more flexible, moulting periodically to upsize its armour.

~

go, releasing underwatertalk in small explosions: here nothing is yet irreparably broken, and

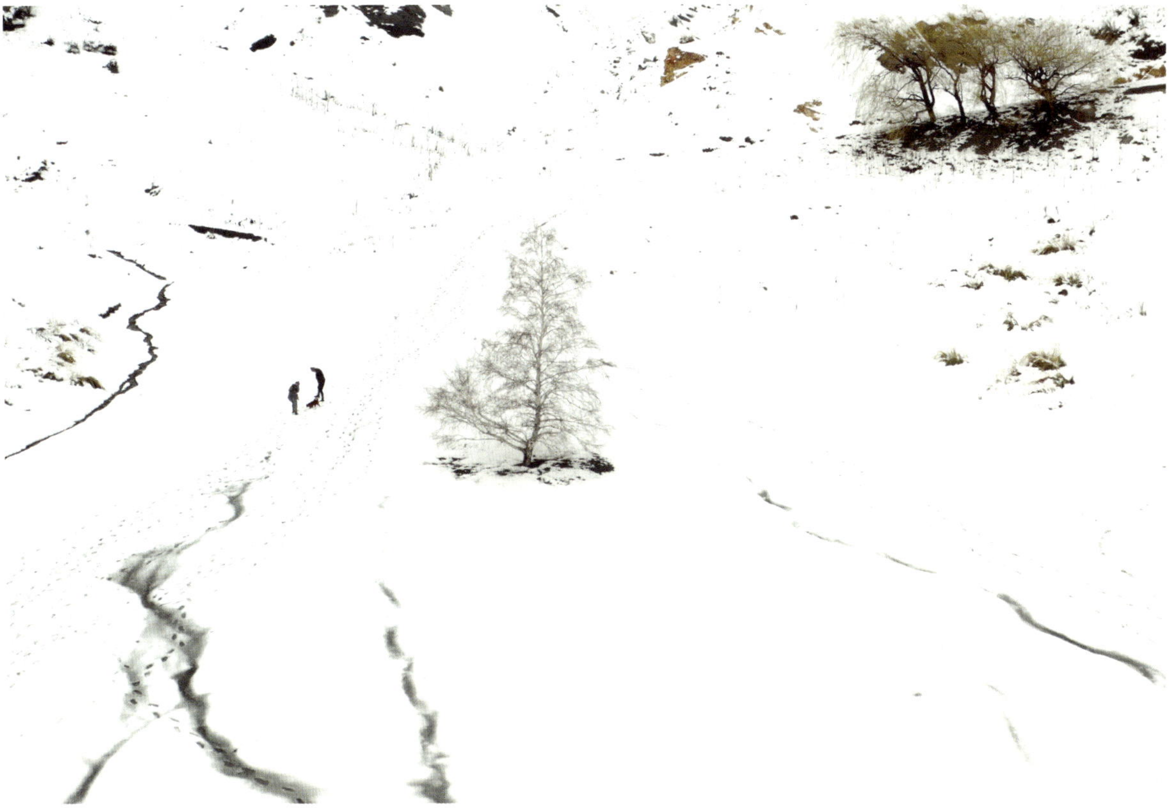

silence is restorative. Below, old gods still navigate time-tested stories, while above, the gods of

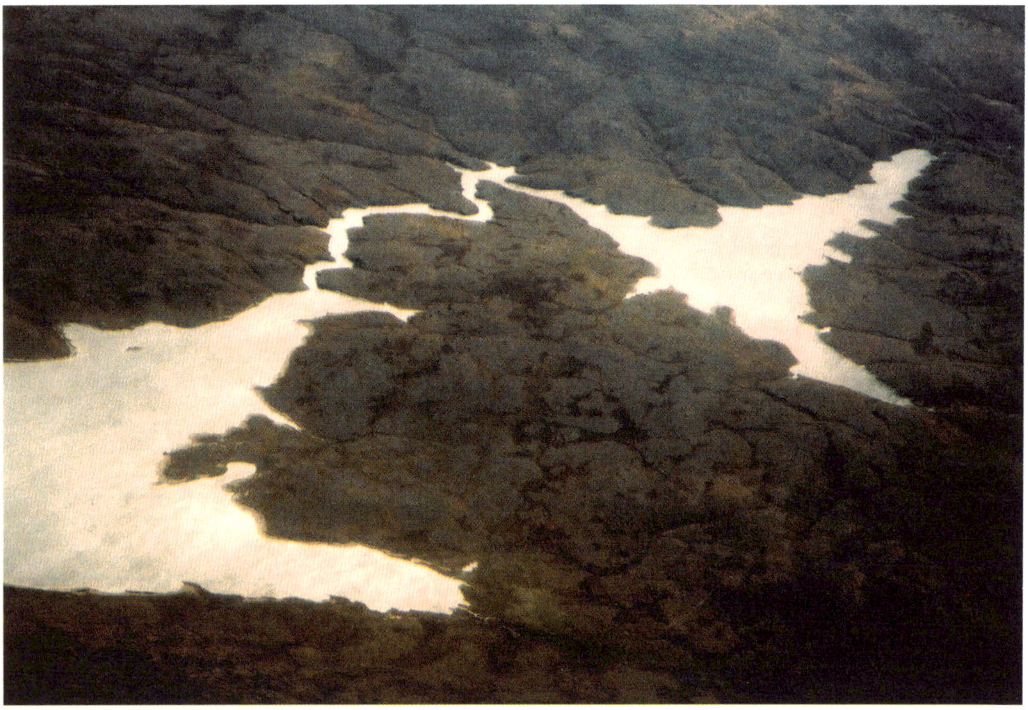

speed and plenty whose turn it was to rule have lost the plot. I can't talk underwater, that's why it's

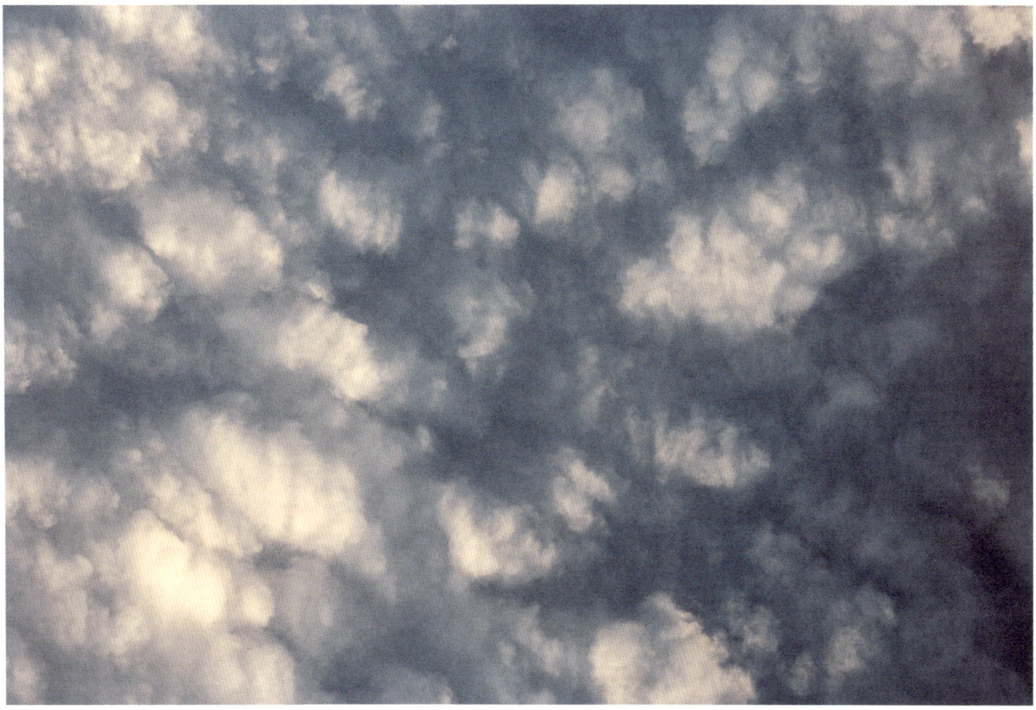

'A profound thought is in a constant state of becoming; it adopts the experience of a life and assumes its shape,' writes Albert Camus. An artist's creative output 'is strengthened in its successive and multiple aspects: his works. One after another they complement one another, correct or overtake one another, contradict one another, too.' This thought appears in *The Myth of Sisyphus*, Camus' attempt to determine once and for all the correct response to Hamlet's famous question in the face of the pointlessness and humiliations of human existence: is the better part of valour *to be, or not to be*, when after all *he himself might his quietus make / With a bare bodkin?* Or, in Camus' own formulation, 'Does the absurd dictate death?'

~

so refreshing .... The darkness down here is larger by far than the world of breathable air or the

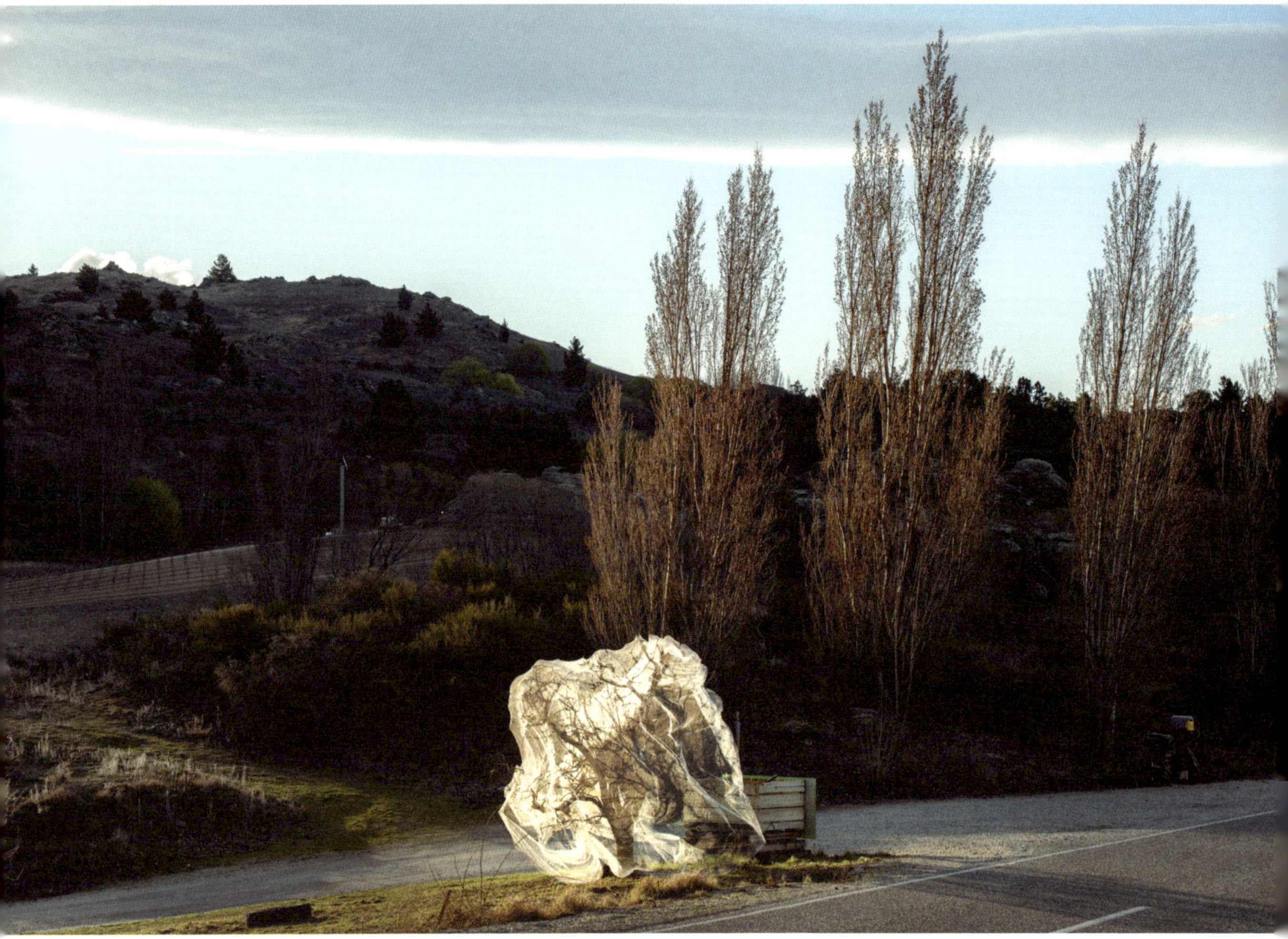

inner space of the skull. In the bathysphere I sit quite still, and through its fused quartz eye watch

King Sisyphus fostered both navigation and commerce. In one tradition, says Camus, he was wise and prudent, but in another he was 'disposed to practice the profession of highwayman' by plundering the ships that plied his waters. Zeus ordered Thanatos to chain up the robber king down in Tartarus, the lowest realm of the underworld — but Sisyphus the cunning turned the tables by imprisoning Thanatos instead, so that for a time no human being could be killed. (*Death, thou shalt die.*) The gods could not tolerate this, for it rather spoiled the fun of battle to leave no corpses.

~

A painted lobster is the second that comes to mind. The painter was Tupaia, the master sea artist (period term for a navigator) of Ra'iātea who guided Captain Cook on his 1769 expedition throughout the Pacific Islands, then travelled on with him to New Zealand and Australia. In New Zealand, Tupaia painted a triple portrait that shows a cloaked Māori figure handing a lobster over to a European in coat and hat. We can assume that, as an item of trade, the lobster was not given a pet name, but today we can identify it as one of the *Palinuridae*, the clawless family of spiny lobsters that play the violin.

~

the animated constellations of the deep go by: the anglerfish, the viperfish with flash of sabre teeth,

Palinurus, from whom this family takes its name, was Aeneas's pilot and, like Tupaia, an experienced navigator. But one night, as Aeneas and his Trojans were sailing towards Italy, Palinurus fell asleep at the wheel (*the darkness sur- / rounds us*) and tumbled overboard. He survived drowning to be washed ashore four days later, but was swiftly murdered by the brutish locals, who left him naked and unburied on the beach.

~

the silver hatchetfish, the barbel, and the squid looking back at me from behind its shining eyes

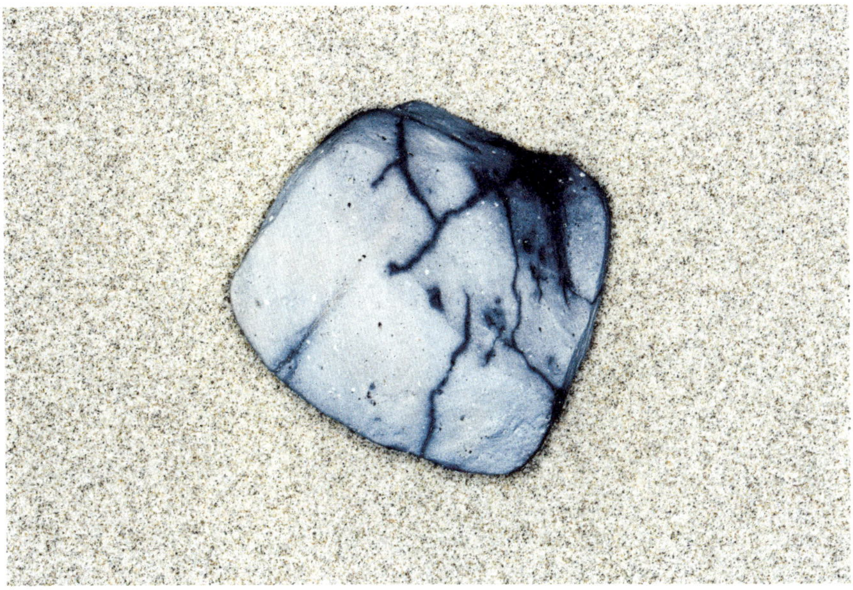

ringed with coloured lights, the elegant engineering of the flying snails, the pale-green photophores

All creation is ended by blind fate, says Camus. 'If something brings creation to an end, it is not the victorious and illusory cry of the blinded artist: "I have said everything," but the death of the creator which closes his experiences and the book of his genius.'

~

Instead of claws, Palinurids have very long antennae with thick, spiny bases that are sometimes used to club or pincer prey. Most family members have a flattened and ridged protuberance misleadingly called the 'plectrum' at the base of the antennae. Rather than functioning like a guitar pick, as the name suggests, the lobster's plectrum serves as a kind of violin bow, producing sound by friction: when drawn across the 'file', a lump covered in microscopic scales or shingles near the lobster's eye, it produces a loud, raspy buzz or squeak, which scientists believe is meant to warn off predators.

~

of lanternfish, the dragonfish whose passing I recognise by the twin row of lights on its side like

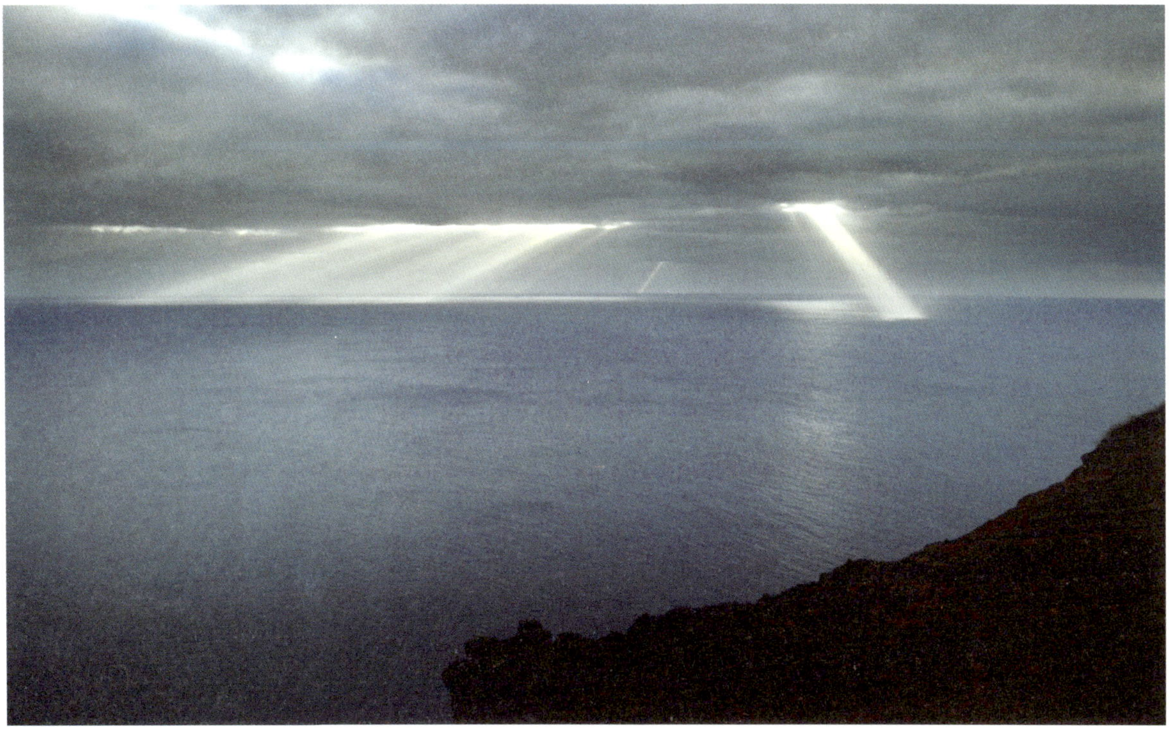

the windows of a submarine passenger jet. I try to hold my breath so as not to fog the glass. One

'To be true,' writes Camus, 'a succession of works can be but a series of approximations of the same thought. But it is possible to conceive of another type of creator proceeding by juxtaposition. Their words may seem to be devoid of inter-relations, to a certain degree, they are contradictory. But viewed all together, they resume their natural groupings. From death, for instance, they derive their definitive significance.' The lobster moults, and must hide while its new carapace hardens. During this period, however, it can still play the violin in self-defence. 'But perhaps the great work of art has less importance in itself than in the ordeal it demands of a man and the opportunity it provides him of overcoming his phantoms and approaching a little closer to his naked reality.' In the twenty-first century we can take objections to the artist's gender as read, but perhaps this kind of heroism does have a peculiarly masculine cast.

~

gorgeous light big as a sixpence comes steadily towards me, then explodes in a hundred brilliant

Camus takes a moment to decry the 'thesis-novel', a work that is 'inspired by a *smug* thought' and written 'to demonstrate the truth you feel sure of possessing'. Ideas, he says, are the contrary of thought. 'Those I am speaking of or whom I imagine are, on the contrary, lucid thinkers. At a certain point where thought turns back on itself, they raise up the images of their works like the obvious symbols of a limited, mortal and rebellious thought.' The spiny lobster's tail flicks under its body to propel it backwards when under attack. The sound of its violin-playing may be a warning to predators, but the lobster itself is deaf to its own music.

~

Tupaia's lobster would almost certainly have belonged to the Palinurid species now known as *Jasus edwardsii*, the red rock lobster. It is one of the *silentes*, that small group of spiny lobsters who do not play the violin, for they lack the equipment.

Jasus caveorum, edwardsii, frontalis, lalandii, paulensis, tristani.

~

points, super nova in the deep blue-black saltwater night. I am an embryo unborn in this aurora

Lobsters come conveniently packaged for trade. The specimen Tupaia depicted was passed hand to hand in a transaction in which there was nothing for the lobster but death. In the watercolour, the lobster is tethered with a flax cord rather than a silk ribbon. The cord suspends it in mid-air like a child's wind-up toy being reluctantly shared. The figure about to receive this living food parcel wears a black frock coat with silver frogging, grey breeches, stockings and black shoes. One of his hands extends forwards to grasp the creature, whose antennae point directly at him. The other seems to have a napkin draped over its outstretched palm, like a black-clad waiter in a formal dining establishment that might feature *homard à l'Américaine* on its menu. History records, however, that the cloth being proffered in exchange was tapa cloth, a much stiffer proposition than a table napkin. Its colour is not white but sandy.

For several centuries the Māori, the lobster and the waiter were anonymous, but in 1998 the waiter finally acquired his true name. He was in fact Joseph Banks, gentleman scientist at the time of Cook's voyage, later president of the Royal Society –

Nay, he upon societies who thought,
To learning's stock a deal of treasure brought,
Dragging Obscurity so deep to day:
Making the dame turn out her bag,
Conceal'd beneath her inky cloak . . .

~

maris .... Up top, the mountains rocks cobbles and pebbles lend the stream its phonemes as it passes

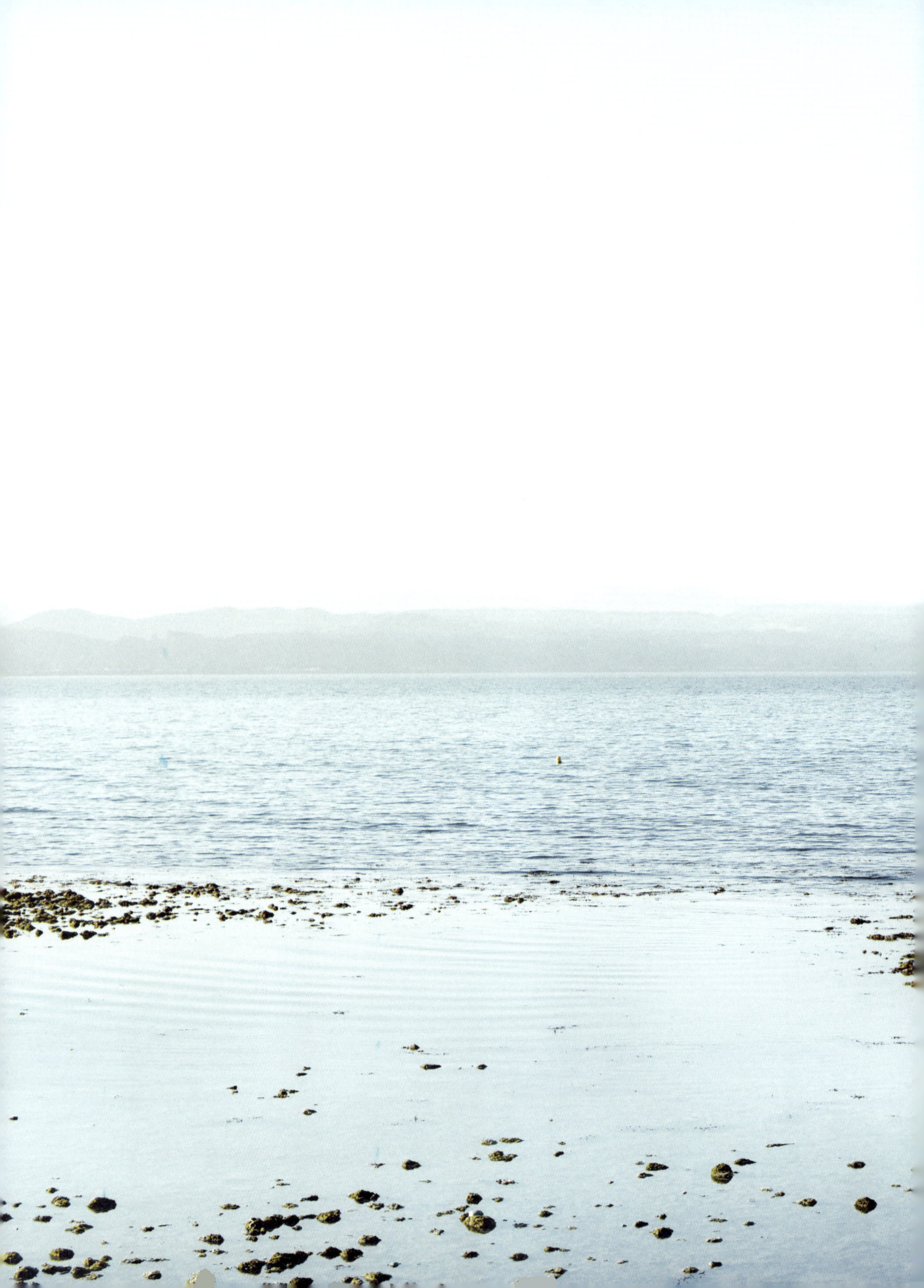

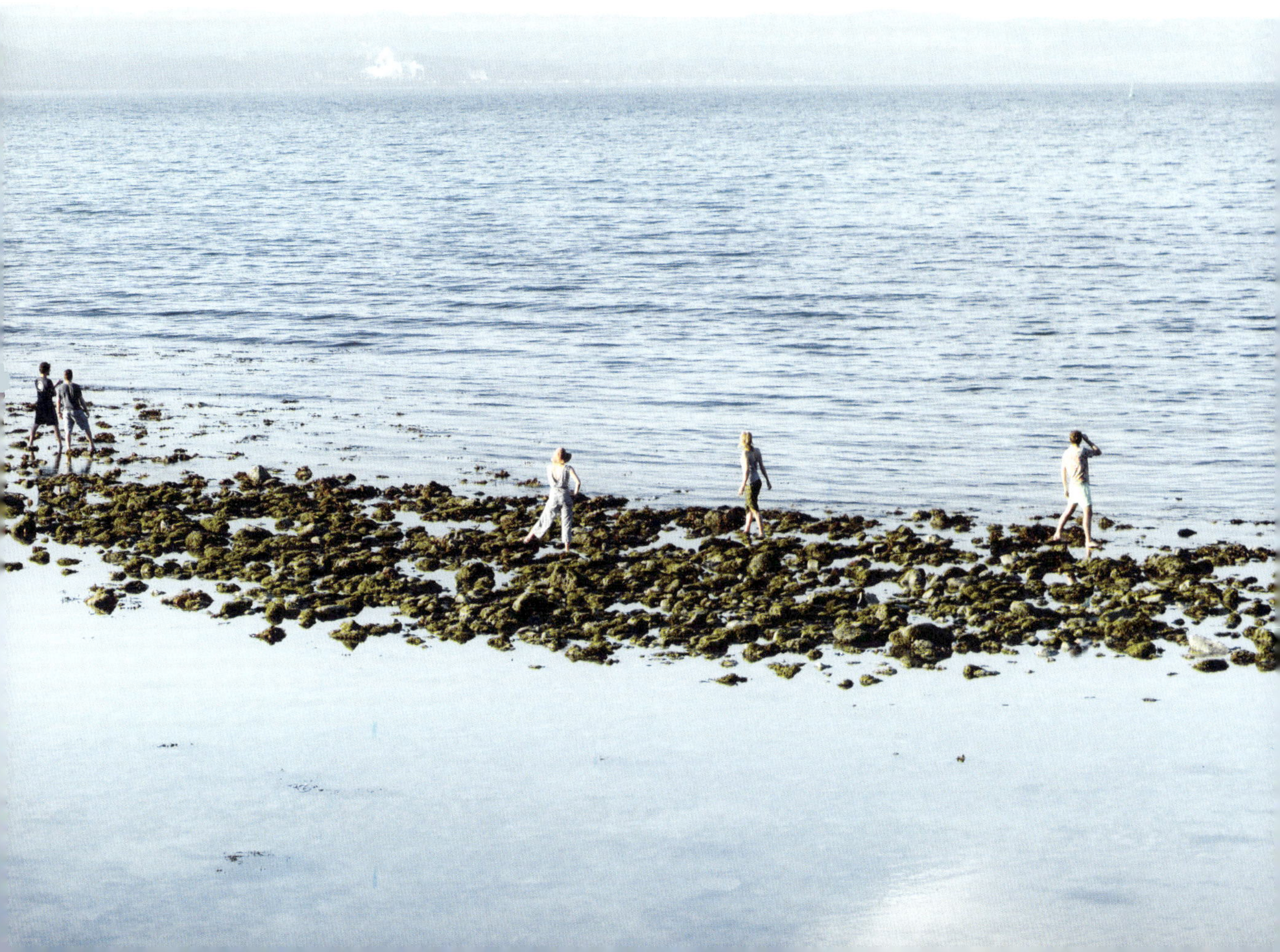

In Nerval's day the French zoologist Henri Milne Edwards (his father was English) produced his three-volume *History of Crustacea*, which became the standard text on the subject. Milne Edwards held senior positions at the Paris Museum, the Jardin des Plantes and the Sorbonne, and he pioneered scuba diving with an air pump, a modified fireman's helmet, and lead sandals that enabled him to walk on the seafloor in Sicily, and observe and collect specimens there. It was he who christened the packhorse lobster, New Zealand's other lobster species, *Palinurus verreauxi*. (One hundred and sixty years and several taxonomic shifts later, this lobster has its own genus, *Sagmariasus verreauxi.*)

~

through the throats of earth and stone; rain snow and ice all give it volume. Handfuls of fear are

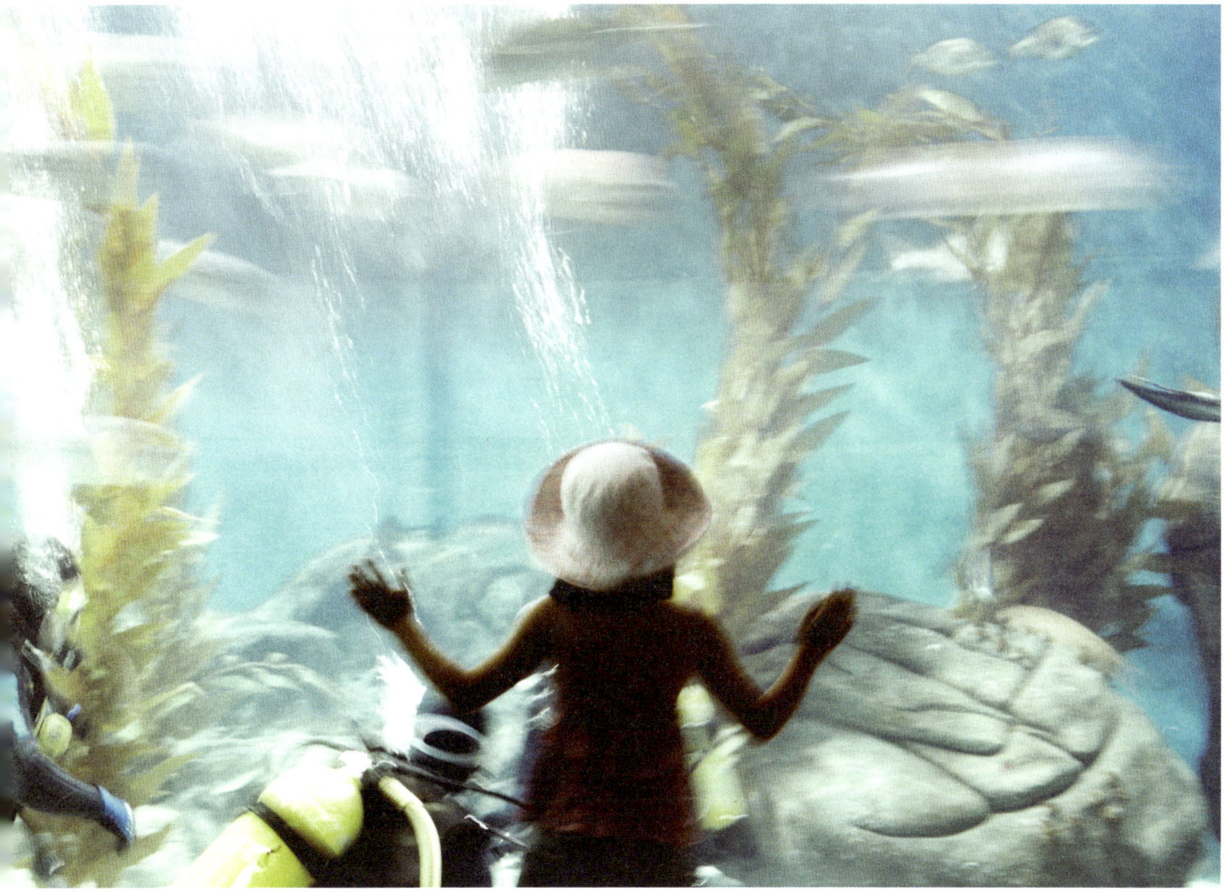

everywhere found in dust, but this is water — either a hymn or a disaster, and between the two

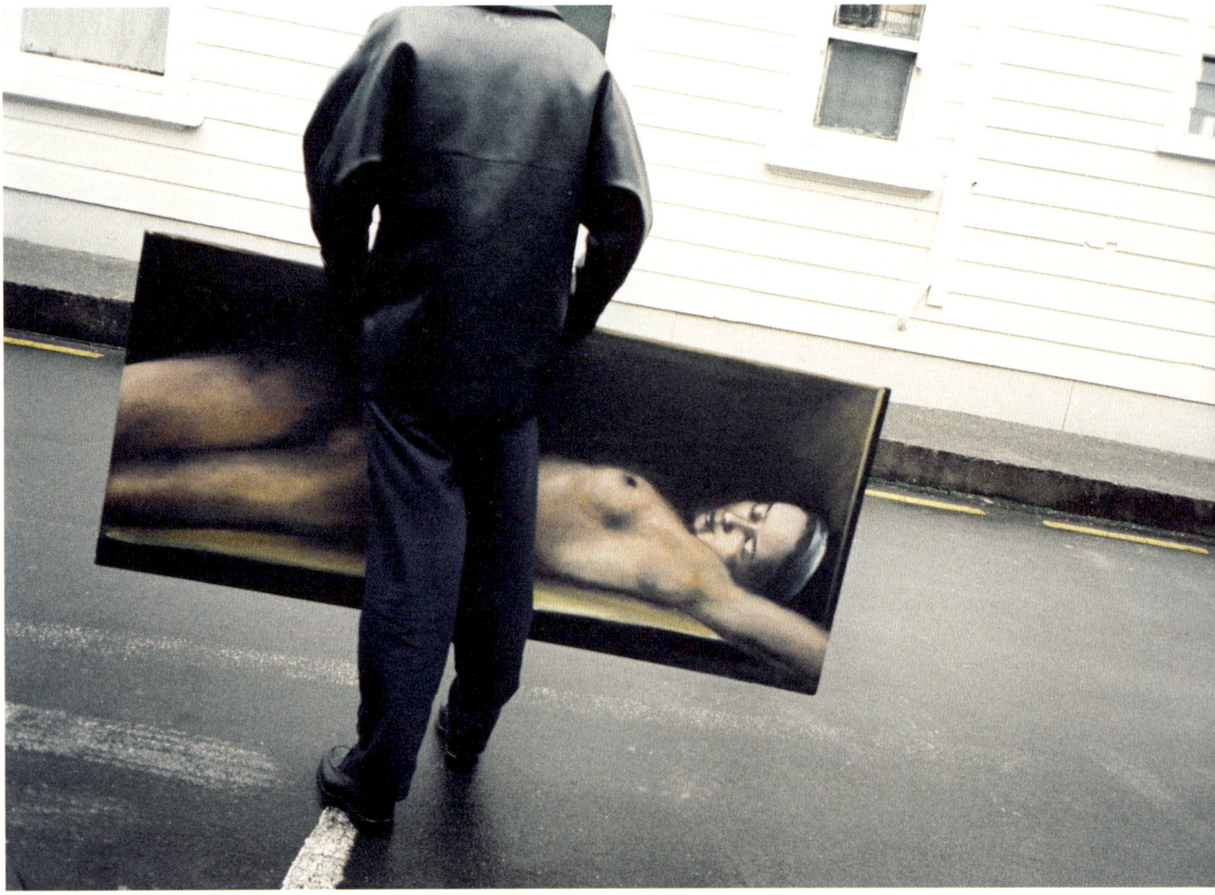

a bright transparent whispergiggletrickle or a muddy, invasive tale told by creatures whose way

The Linnaean name for Tupaia's lobster, *Jasus edwardsii*, was selected in honour of Henri's son Alphonse, who was also a student of the spiny lobster. While *Jasus* are mostly stay-at-homes, not venturing further than five kilometres, some populations migrate up to a hundred kilometres, and at least one is known to have travelled four hundred and sixty kilometres. It is now believed that lobsters are 'true navigators' — that is, they use the Earth's magnetic field to determine their position. This despite the fact that their nervous systems are not complex. Boundaries are useful to classification, but some will always stray beyond them.

In New Zealand, lobsters are more commonly referred to as crayfish, although strictly speaking the word 'crayfish' (*Paranephrops planifrons* and *P. zealandicus*) applies only to the native freshwater species or 'koura', the word for lobster entered in Banks's Māori vocabulary list, assembled no doubt with Tupaia's help. Unlike the lobsters found in New Zealand's coastal waters, kōura have claws, as European lobsters do.

~

of staying alive could choke the local into extinction .... I transplanted my alien weeping to this

The lobster is a solitary creature, a crevice dweller that prefers darkness – but not always. There are times when it needs to be found, or to congregate. The negotiation of hiding and finding will determine its longevity. A lobster in the Monaco aquarium is as old as I am, perhaps older.

According to a Slavic proverb, 'The young lobster learns his manner of walking from the old lobster.' When they go out walking in their natural habitat, young *Jasus* lobsters are at risk from the appetites of cod, sea bream, wrasse, scorpion fish, conger eels, small sharks and octopuses – and each other. Their elders need fear only the larger sharks, and grouper. Although eating the young means eating the future, eating an ancestor, for reasons I can't quite explain, seems the far greater crime.

~

land where it took root on riverbanks and went wild. Fast-forward to rivers that paint their decay

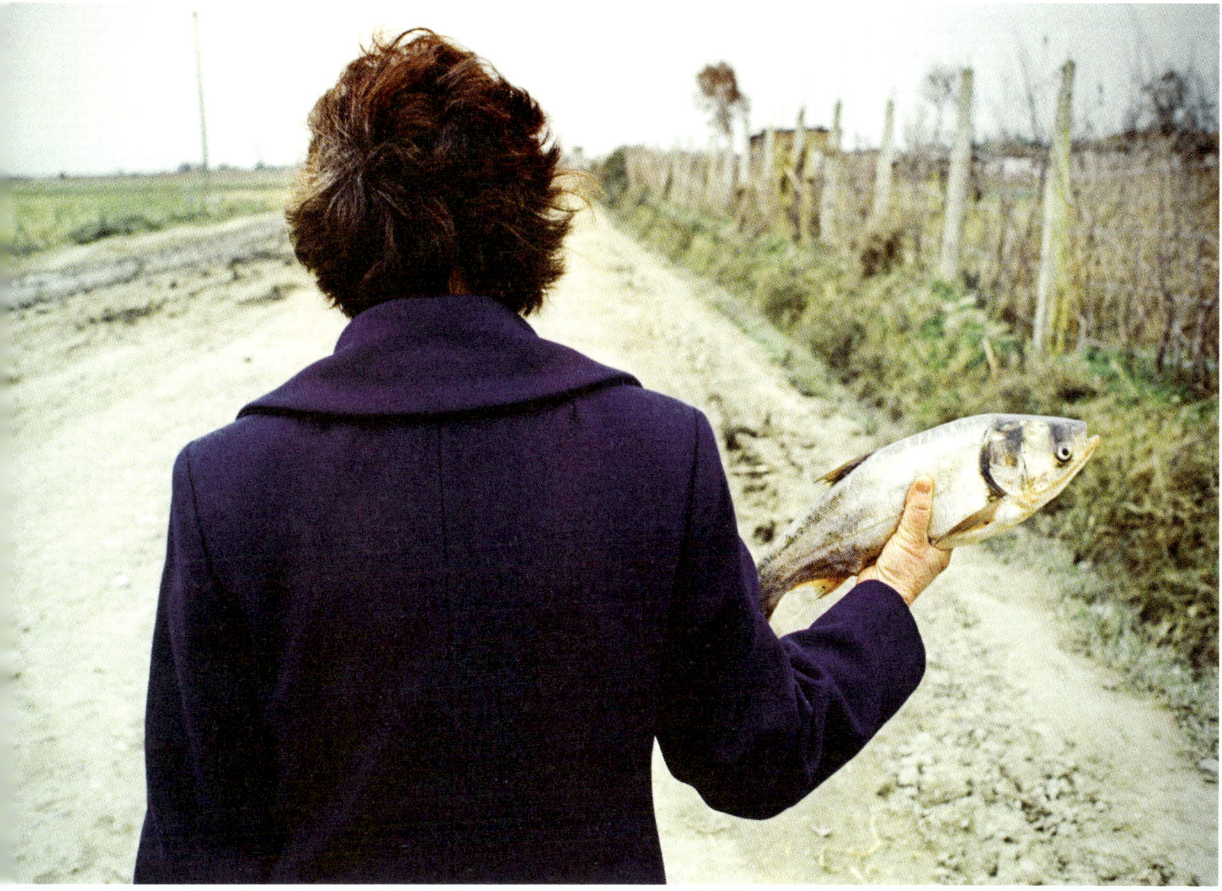

in virulent chemical watercolours or spread in vast flat water-acres. Even underwater gods need

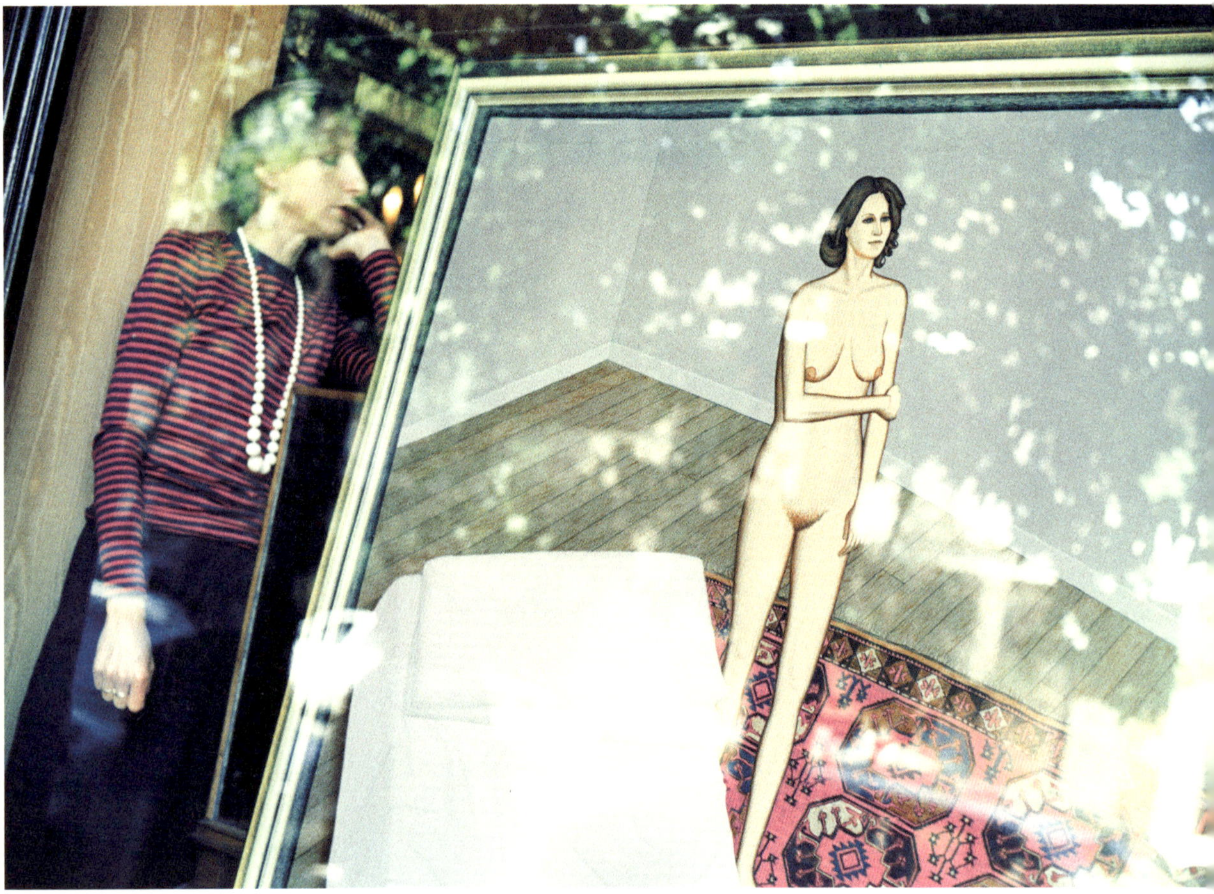

oxygen, but fire is hungry for it too, and I have given all the oxygen to fire and food. It's a sorry

Hunger for the unobtainable leads to voyaging, but virtual geography knows no boundaries. Concerning the secrets of the sea: the migration of the Caribbean lobster is on display in the international aquarium of YouTube. Who would have guessed that they are such elegant and collaborative sprinters? How satisfying it is to have seen them travel. And yet –

If all secrets can be discovered without voyaging, what becomes of longing? Perpetual hunger is a fate to be avoided, but there is also discomfort in being perpetually replete. Some voyages are undertaken to bring things to light; most are made with the intention of disclosure. Of Milne Edwards it is recorded that 'he did not hesitate to risk his life' on the underwater walks from which he brought back news of the seafloor and its inhabitants.

~

truth that even this paper is complicit, the pages carrying both dream and reason; our making

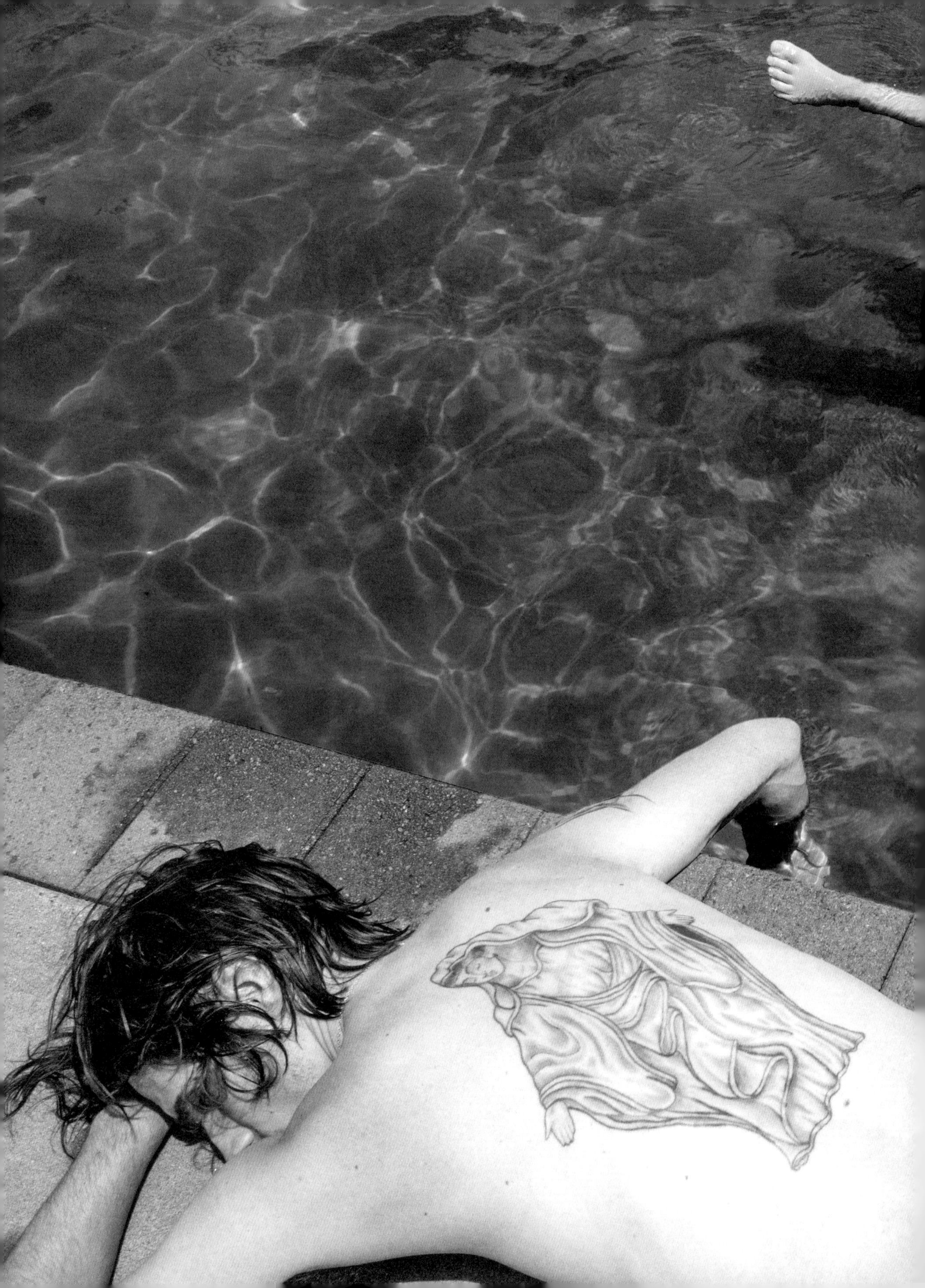

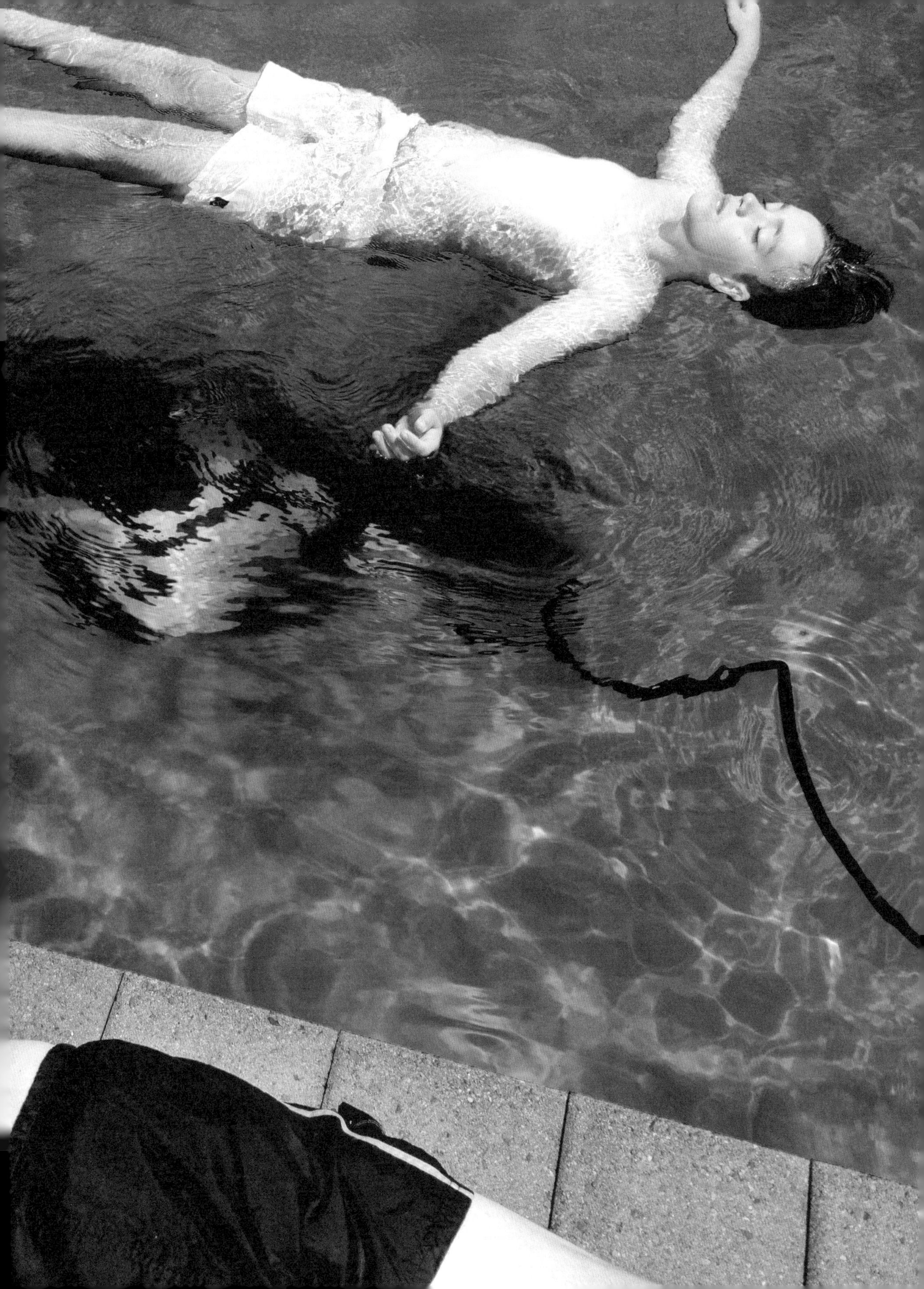

In 1944, a book of autobiographical fragments called *The Unquiet Grave* was published under the nom de plume Palinurus. The book took its title from a ballad in which a young man mourns for his dead lover by sitting on her grave 'for a twelve-month and a day', but much of it is a paean of nostalgia for a period of married happiness spent in sunny pre-war France, a happiness subsequently wrecked (although the book doesn't tell us so) by its author's marital infidelity, which is repented here at leisure.

Our literary Palinurus claims that among his previous incarnations — which include a lemur, a melon, and Aristippus (a hedonistic philosopher who was also shipwrecked) — he has been a lobster, and he invokes his crustacean avatar as a friendly spirit guide on his dive into the underwater world of depression: 'Ancestor, my old incarnation, O *Palinurus Vulgaris*, the Venetian red crawfish, langouste, or rock-lobster, whether feeding upon the spumy Mauretanian Banks, or undulating — southward to Tenerife, northward to Scilly — in the systole and diastole of the wave: free me from guilt and fear, free me from guilt and fear, dapple-plated scavenger of the resounding sea!'

~

floats on a polluting medium .... On land the words were lost that let me appreciate how water

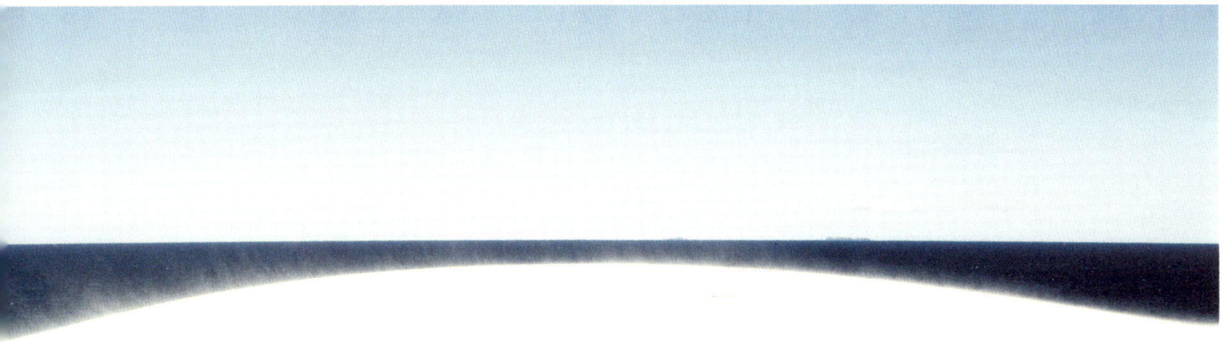

thinks in collaboration with its creatures who take on the colouration of their thought-bed and serve

Tupaia's picture resembles an equation or a diagram, with the lobster as some previously unconceived mathematical sign that mediates between the two human figures. It is not a plus sign, although that is one function of the encounter. Nor an equals sign, although from a contemporary viewpoint it's tempting to read it that way. The lobster is a third term, mysterious yet nonetheless verifiable, and external to both parties, something they can point to and agree upon in their calculations about one another. It is the beginning of a shared language. It both connects the figures and distances them. If there were a Buddhist mathematics, it might define this term as 'not two, not one'.

~

as moving nouns, being indivisible from doing, the whole of place and thing a movement in which

'Any thought that abandons unity glorifies diversity,' writes Camus. 'And diversity is the home of art.' Joseph Banks and his companion Daniel Solander, a Swede who had studied under Linnaeus himself, would glorify the diversity of the species they collected on their Pacific journey in their magnificent *Florilegium*, based on the drawings of Cook's other artist, Sydney Parkinson. None of them lived to see the *Florilegium* finished, however — the first complete, full-colour edition did not appear until two hundred years after their voyage. Their botanical specimens had travelled back to England pressed between discarded proofs of *Paradise Lost*. The shared language soon became a largely one-sided conversation.

~

eyes and ears cannot tell the navigator from the navigation .... Without water to both grow and

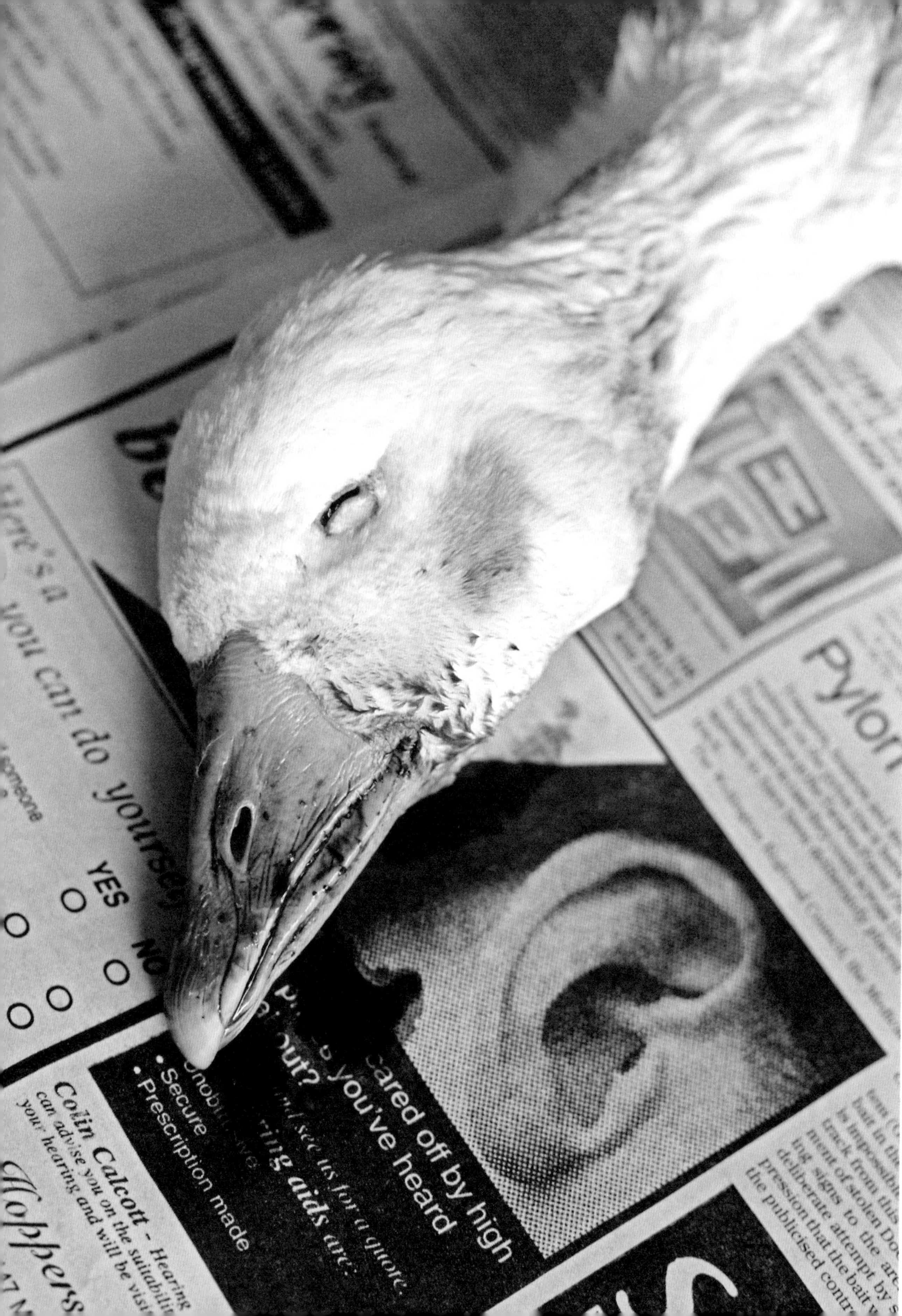

Pylon
you can do
YES
NO
• Secure
• Prescription made
Colin Calcott - Hearing

Foundation Seamounts rock lobster, Cape rock lobster, St Paul rock lobster, Tristan rock lobster // *Justitia longimanus* // African spear lobster, Oriental spear lobster, Japanese spear lobster // musical furry lobster, Indo-Pacific furry lobster // Madagascar Ridge spiny lobster, Cape Verde spiny lobster, Natal spiny lobster, European/common spiny lobster, southern spiny lobster, pink spiny lobster // Asian blunthorn lobster, buffalo blunthorn lobster, American blunthorn lobster, unicorn blunthorn lobster, Japanese blunthorn lobster // Caribbean spiny lobster, Aka-ebi, western rock/spiny lobster, brown spiny lobster, white-whiskered spiny lobster, green spiny lobster, spotted spiny lobster, scalloped spiny lobster, blue spiny lobster, California spiny lobster, Japanese spiny lobster, smoothtail spiny lobster, longlegged spiny lobster, Hawaiian spiny lobster, ornate spiny lobster, Easter Island spiny lobster, pronghorn spiny lobster, mud spiny lobster, royal spiny lobster, Chinese spiny lobster, painted spiny lobster // Chilean jagged lobster, Cape jagged/deepwater lobster // banded whip lobster, red whip lobster, Arabian whip lobster, velvet whip lobster // packhorse/eastern spiny/rock lobster.

~

douse them, words self-immolate, and as weather's even temper shifts key to extreme the pitch and

Lobsters are fearsome, handsome creatures, little living gods of our unconscious, totems of fury and unrepentant strangeness, half-fish, half-insect, living in the liminal space between ocean and pot, taking on their most vivid and attractive colouring only in death, before which they are far better camouflaged. It is painful to see them, as I once did in Oxford's covered market, corralled in a small bare tank with their claws bandaged so they can't damage one another out of stress and ill temper while waiting to be plated. It is painful to see them crammed higgledy-piggledy into a polystyrene box for live export. Pain being a relative term, not susceptible to objective measurement or comparison.

~

yaw of water mirrors the violence of the mind — but when the sirens have fallen silent, the sky with

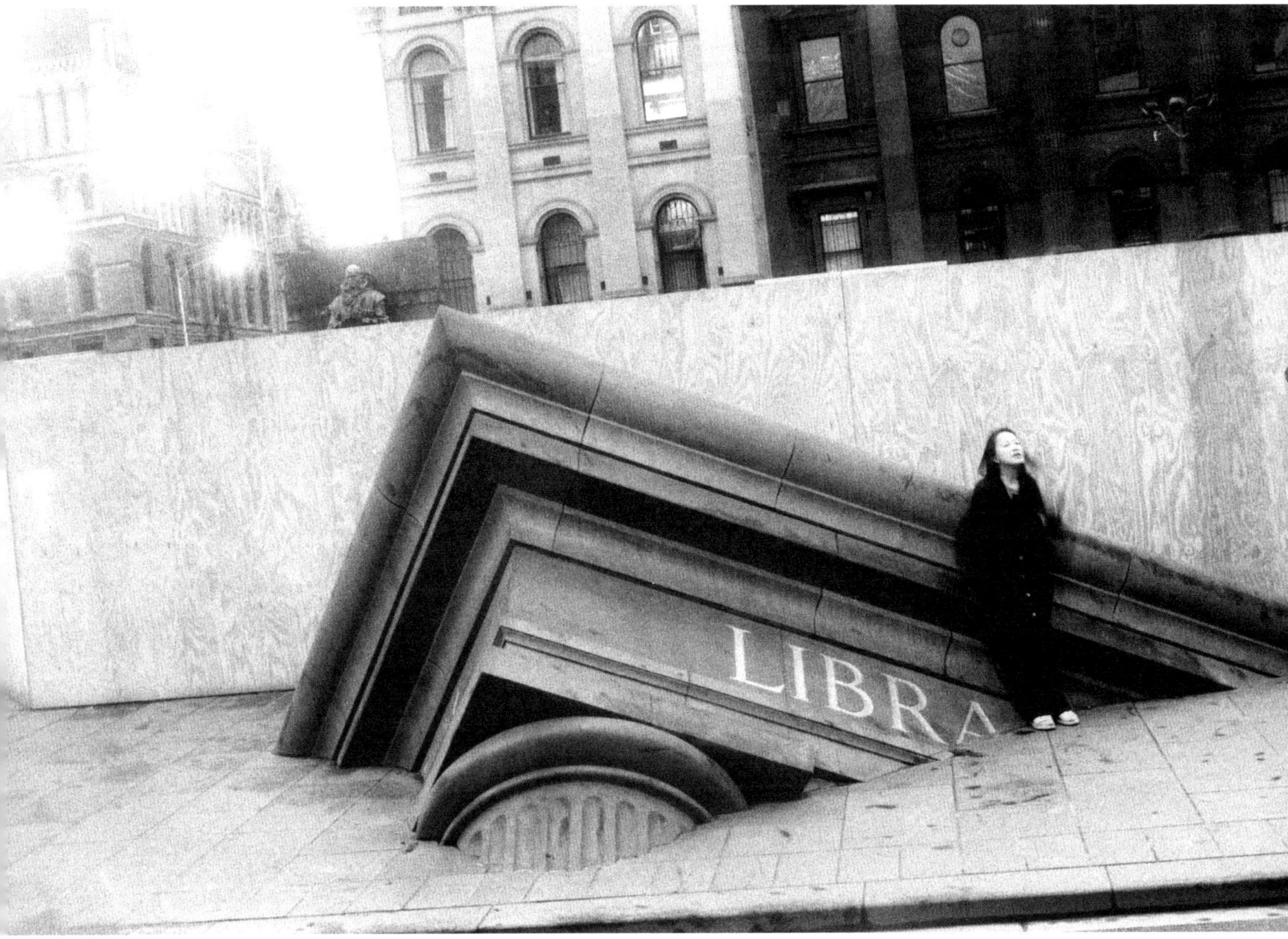

its once infinite messengers will wear a grey uniform. Gods trapped in a museum keep breathing for

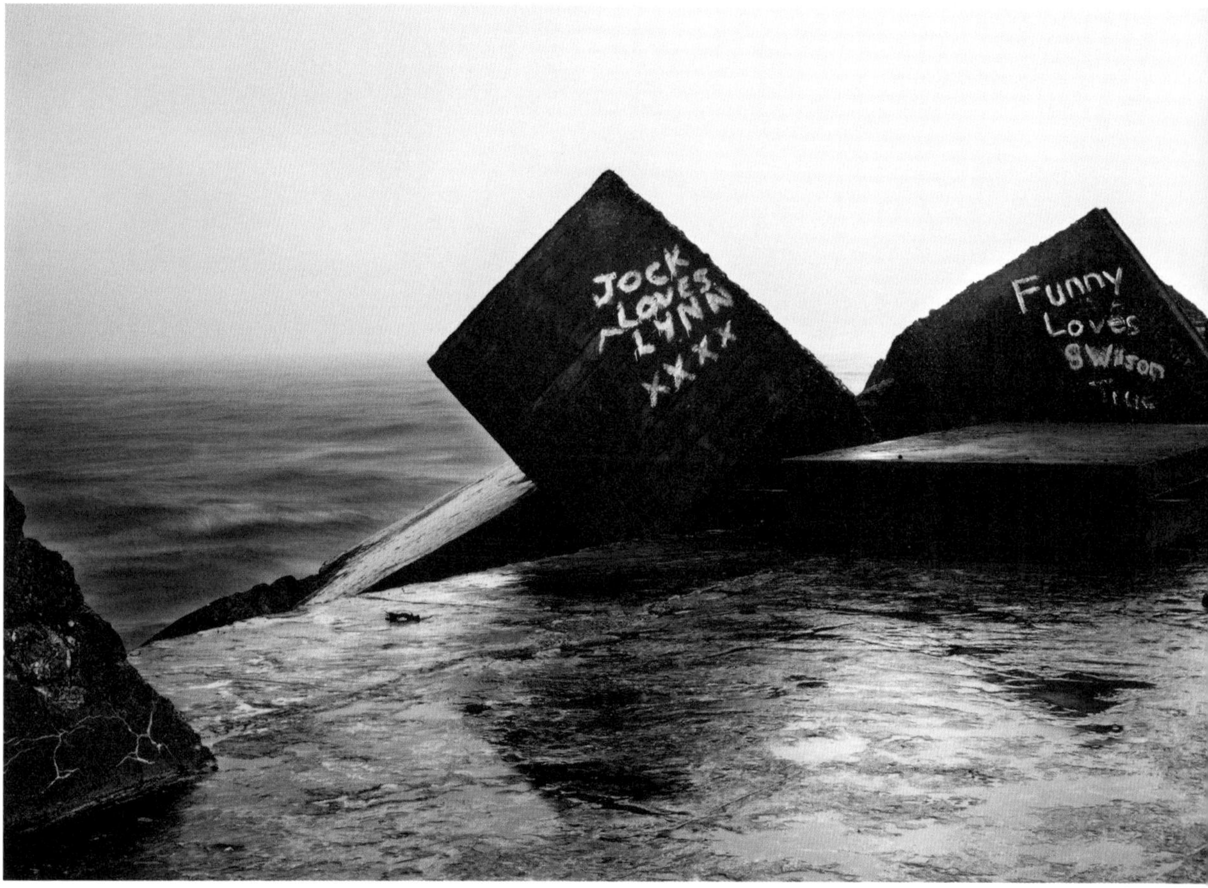

a time, but even the gods are not immortal — that's me again, my wishful thinking . . .

The Solander box or clamshell case is a book form the Swedish botanist invented for the storage of rare and precious maps, manuscripts, books and other documents. The box has a flexible spine that lies flat when open, and the bottom 'lips' slide inside the top lips of the box when it is closed. It may be lined with felt or padded paper.

~

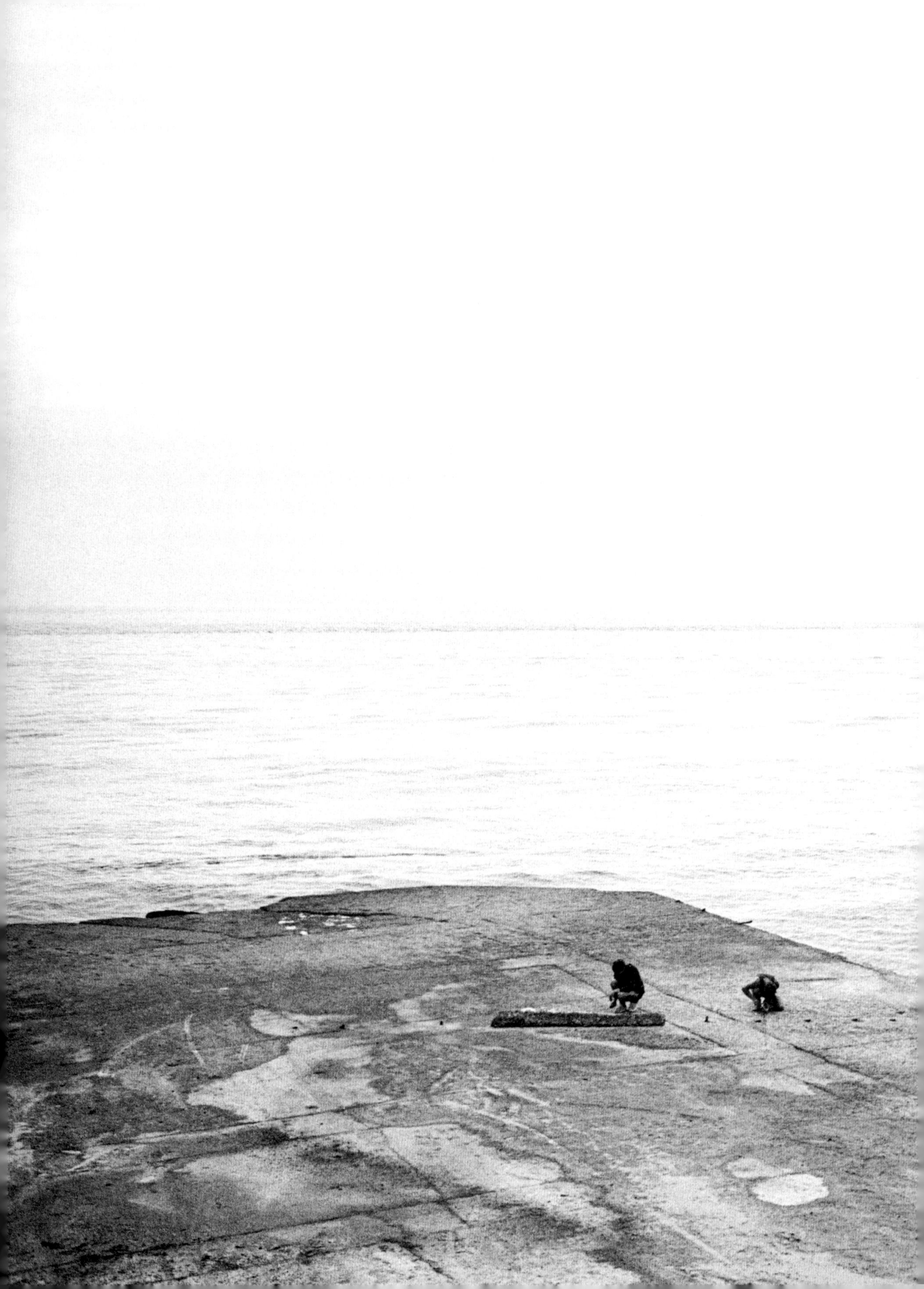

When *The Unquiet Grave* was a success, Palinurus abandoned the thin disguise of his pseudonym and revealed himself to be Cyril Connolly, successful literary editor, serially unsuccessful novelist, chronically melancholy fellow. In the *Aeneid*, the pilot Palinurus nods off at the tiller after he is drugged by the God of Sleep, but Connolly's Palinurus has taken on the colouration of his author's melancholy condition. He does not believe, writes Connolly, that the navigator fell overboard by chance, bad luck or divine intervention. 'Palinurus clearly stands for a certain will-to-failure or repugnance-to-success, a desire to give up at the last moment, an urge towards loneliness, isolation and obscurity. Palinurus, in spite of his great ability and his conspicuous public position, deserted his post in the moment of victory and opted for the unknown shore.'

~

. . . Where you live, kōura are the crusty finite gods of freshwater's infinitive, small green gods who

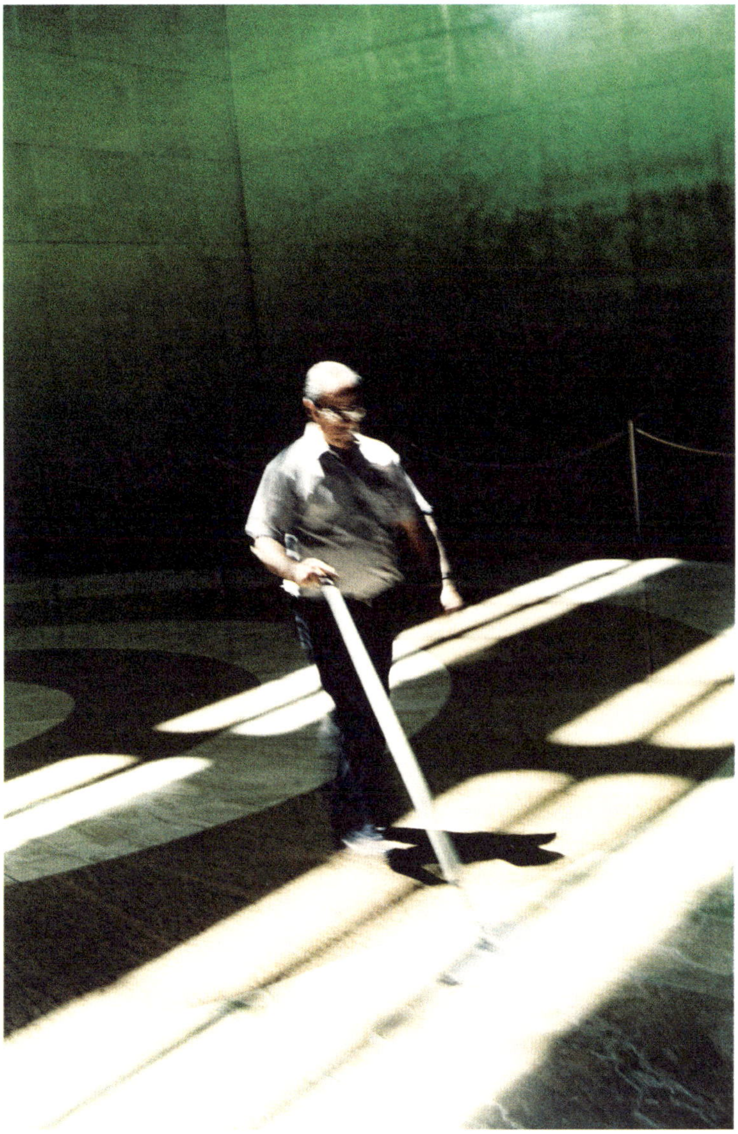

make their modest living in rivers and streams. The kōura want no worshippers, wishing only to be left

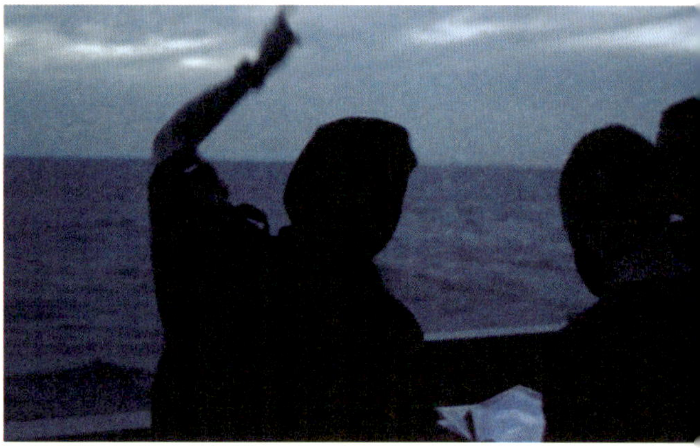

alone with pebbles, nymphs and the flow. Small gods the colour of leaves and stones and light filtered

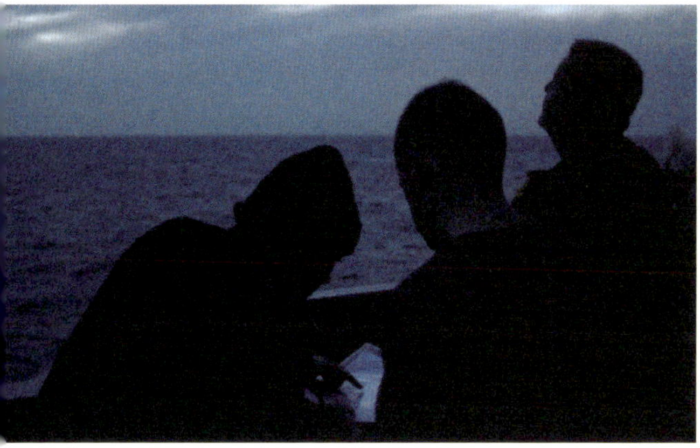 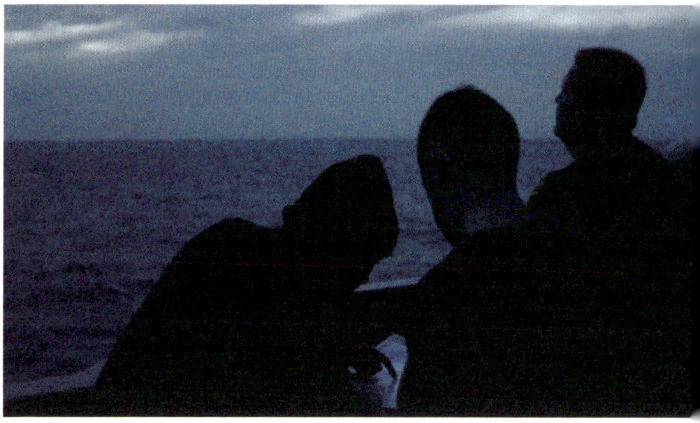

Some voyages are undertaken in pursuit of knowledge, others in hope of profit. Writers might make journeys with no other purpose than to write about them. The writing may be an attempt at the getting of wisdom, but it also has the goal of getting cash. Sometimes intentions are thwarted or reversed. When the privateer Alexander Selkirk set sail around the world he risked his life to acquire wealth, but being cast away on a remote island forced the getting of wisdom upon him instead, and the written account of his experiences is said to have inspired *Robinson Crusoe*, which some regard as the first English novel.

~

through water, invisible to the daylight mind, kōura go verbing at night, while you are still half-blind

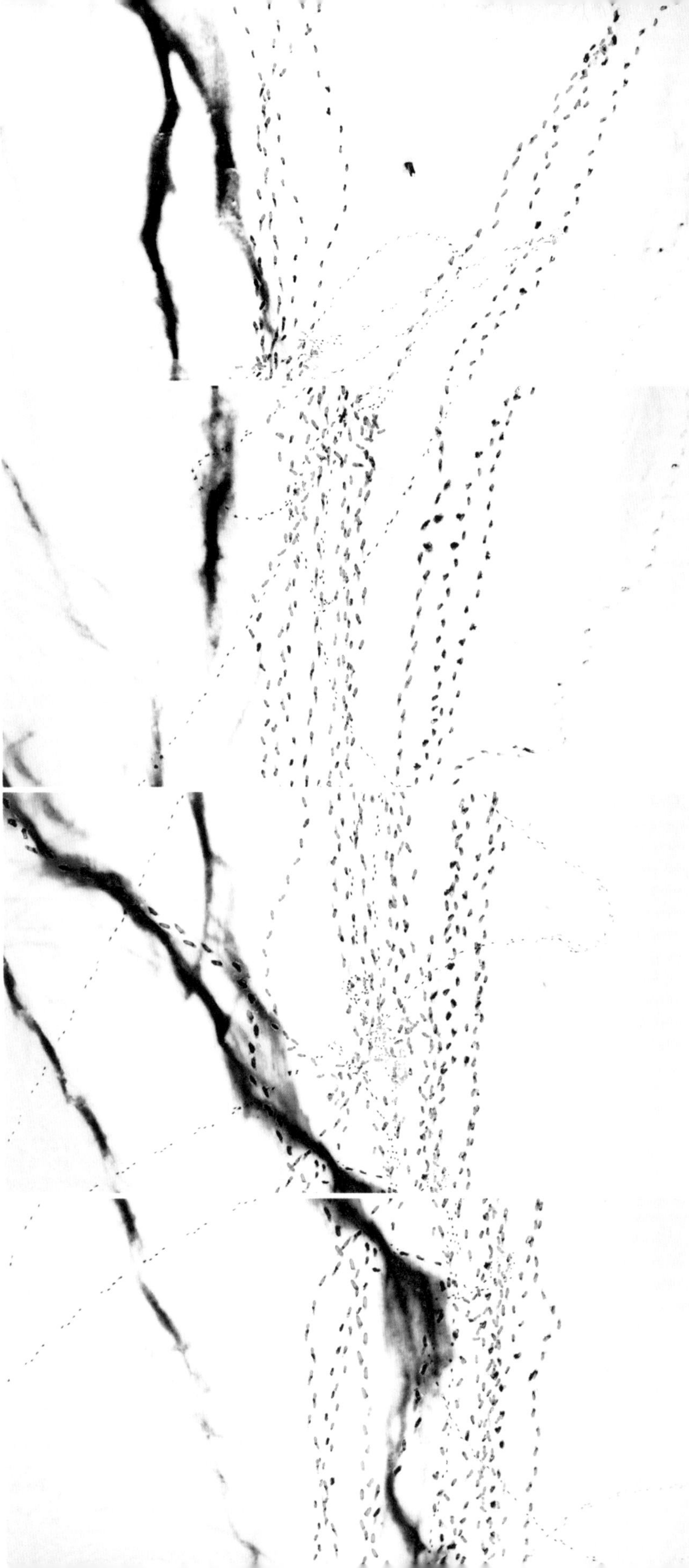

In 2012 the novelist Jonathan Franzen travels to the island of Alejandro Selkirk, off the Chilean coast. Renamed in the 1960s as a ploy to attract tourists, it is still known to the locals as Isla Más Afuera, or The Island Further Away. Franzen's stated purpose is to assuage his discontents in the aftermath of a soul-leaching book tour and to deal with the loss of his friend David Foster Wallace, who had committed suicide in 2008. On the final leg of his journey to the island Franzen travels aboard a lobster boat with some 'adventurous botanists'. In a welcome Wallace might have devised for him, he is greeted on arrival by 'breathtaking quantities of flies' and a 'dozen or so lobsterman shacks huddled at the bottom of a tremendous gorge' from which 'competing boom boxes pumped North and South American music through the open doors . . . pushing back against the oppressive immensity of the gorge and the coldly heaving sea'. The lobstermen are deaf to the whispered tunes of their catch, and Franzen would rather stop his ears against the volume of the world he is hoping to escape.

A man just can't strand himself in the landscape the way he used to. But Franzen is determined to try. He hikes up to one of the island's highest points through a ravine 'lush with maquis, an introduced plant species that is used to repair lobster traps'. He is getting away — as far away as the twenty-first century will allow.

The lobsters that inhabit the coastal waters of Alejandro Selkirk are *Jasus frontalis* and, like their New Zealand relatives, they are *silentes.* In 2001 the minimum legally permissible size for a lobster caught in these waters was 11.5 centimetres, down from 15.5 centimetres in the 1950s. In Selkirk's day, or so Diana Souhami claims in her book on the island, they were three feet long. Lobsters were once 'cheap as chips', as the English say.

~

to the natural history of darkness .... The air under the trees is cool and rich with the inherited wealth

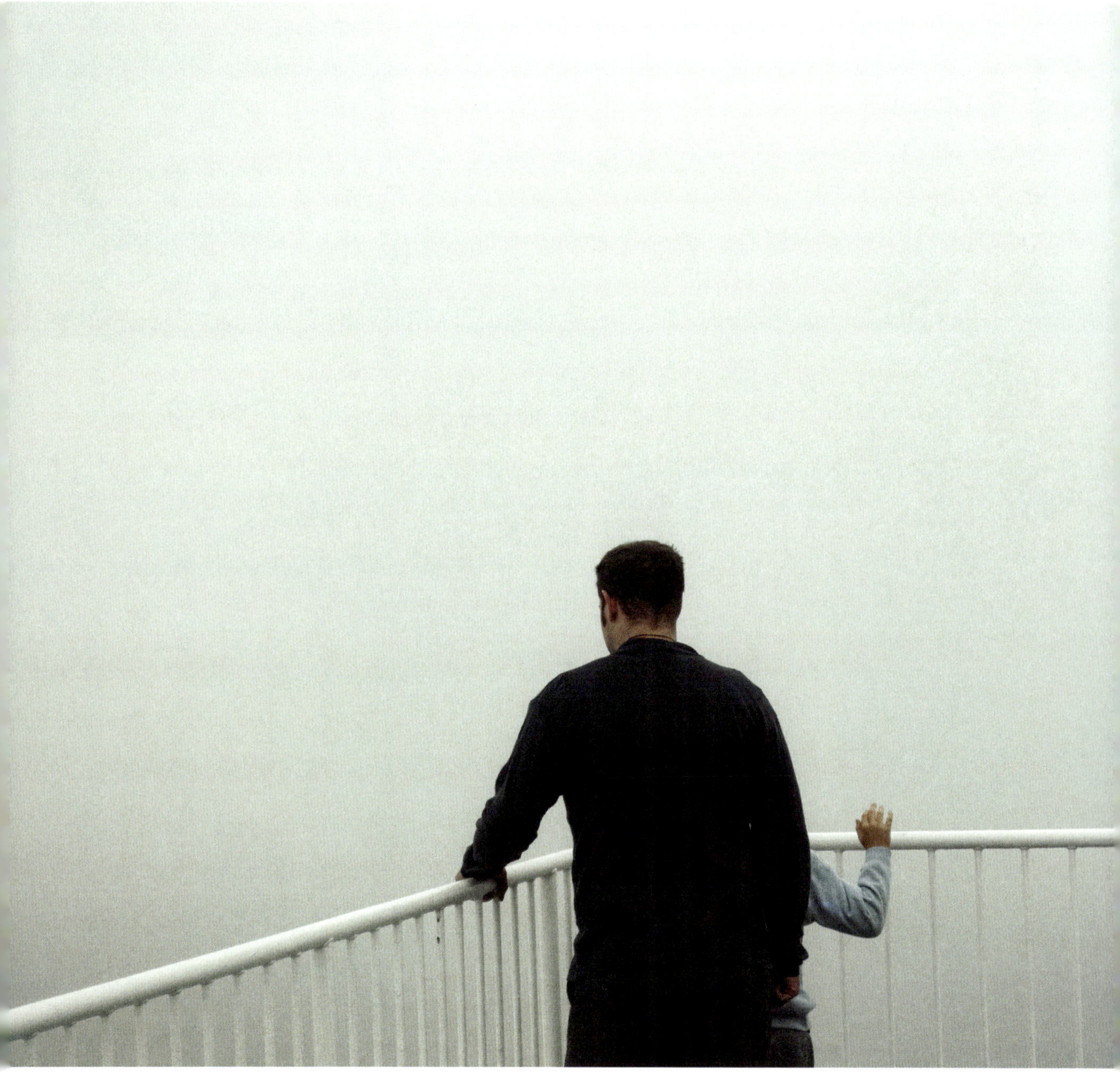

of animals, but kōura are silent in the world of air, they cannot call for rescue. Leaves still drop into the

The first sentence of *The Unquiet Grave*: 'The more books we read, the clearer it becomes that the true function of a writer is to produce a masterpiece and that no other task is of any consequence.' Many writers, Wallace among them, have signed on for that doomed voyage with its ever-receding destination. Like Sisyphus rolling the impossible rock ever upwards, only to watch it roll back down again just as he approaches the summit.

~

The phase box is a simpler form of the Solander box, used to store books while they are being conserved. In an antique wooden matchbox resembling 'a tiny book with a sliding drawer', Franzen carries with him to Más Afuera some of Wallace's ashes.

~

stream for grazing, but a richer food clogs tributaries and fills lakes with green smog from which catfish

Selkirk, sailing master on the privateer *Cinque Ports*, told the ship's captain he would rather be put ashore than sail further on board a ship he deemed unseaworthy. Although Selkirk soon thought better of his decision, the captain took him at his word, put him ashore and sailed on. The worm-eaten *Cinque Ports* was later lost off the coast of Colombia.

~

and perch emerge like submarines to terrorise the indigenes. Light in hidden pools grows mysterious with

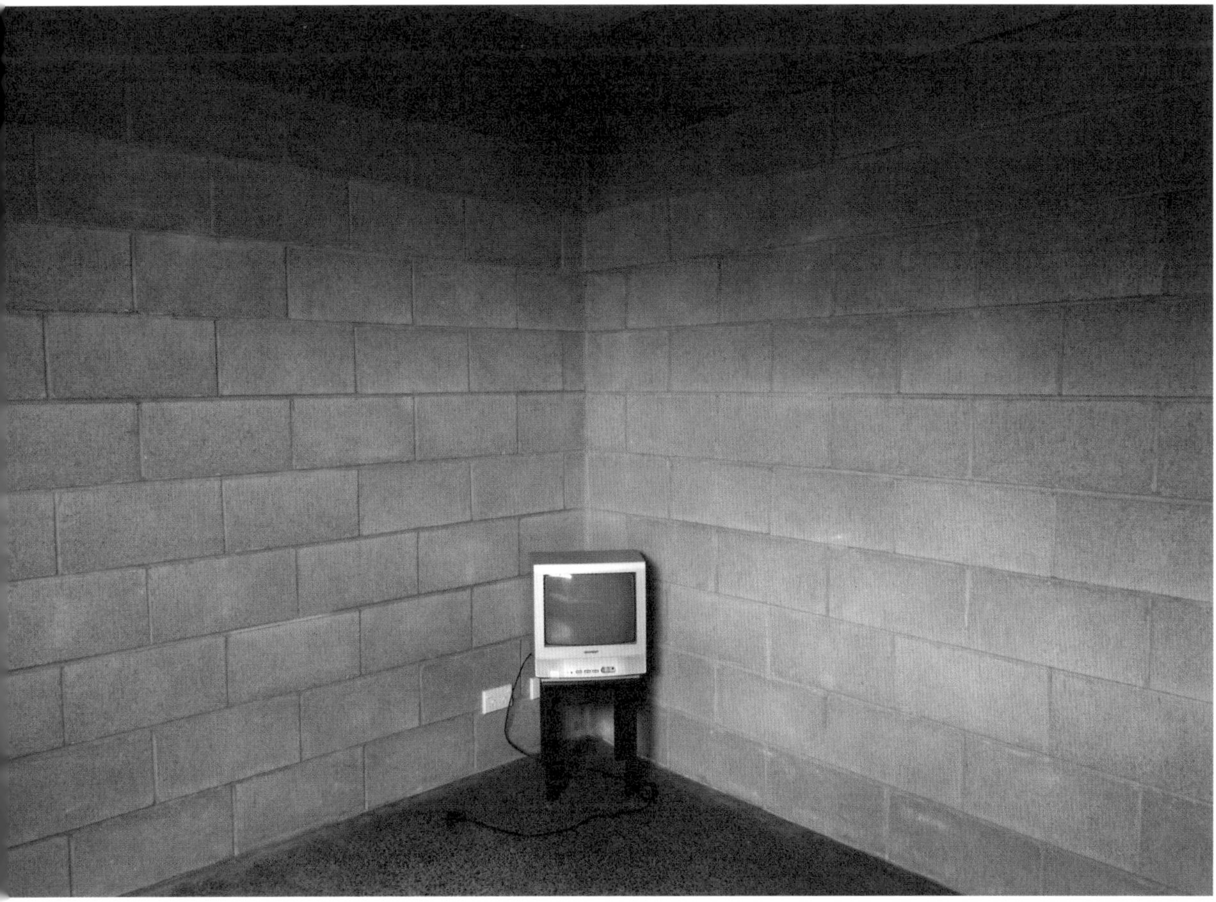

what turns out to be disease, the force-fed earth disgorging rotten juice. Kōura have learned to work

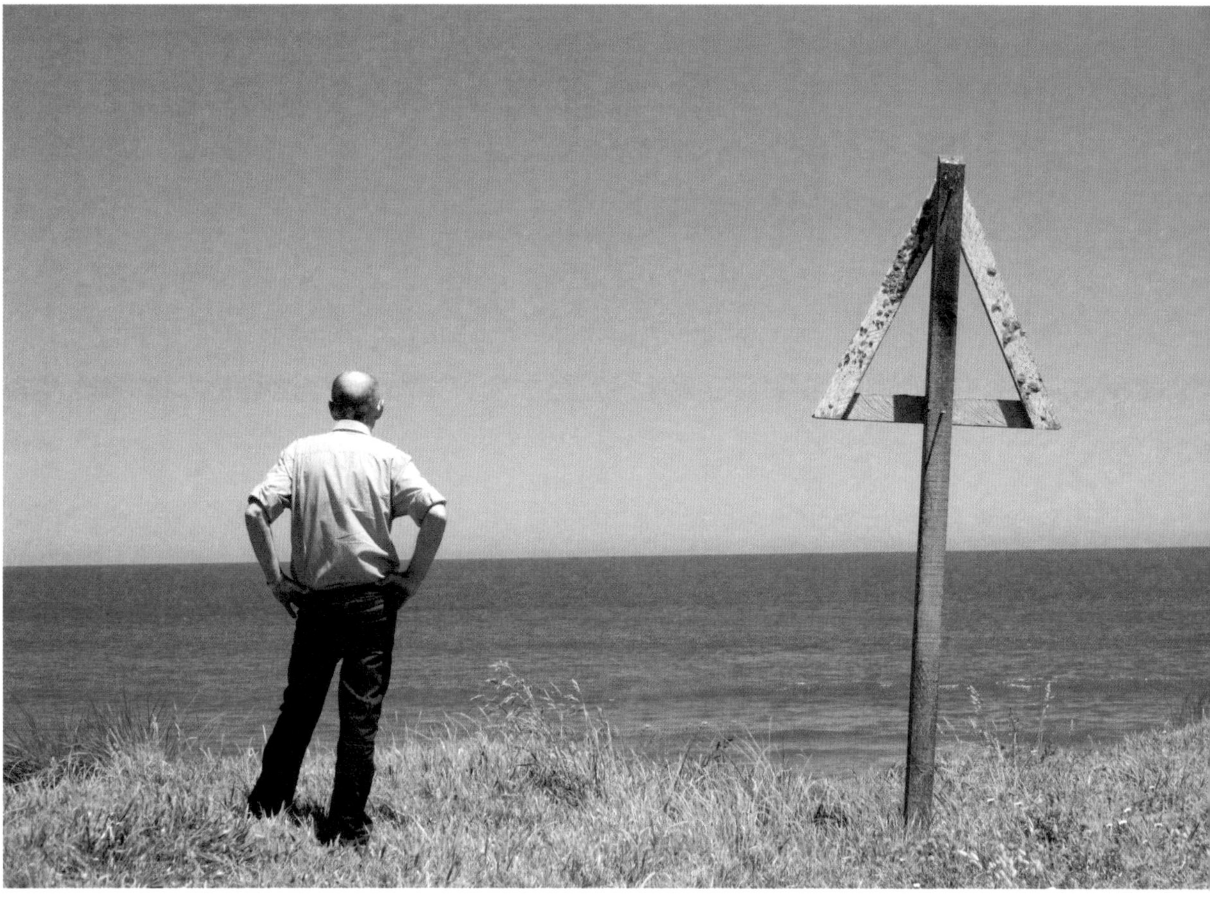

with drought, burrowing into damp mud until the rain returns, but the new floods wash them out of the

When Aeneas visits the underworld, the ghost of Palinurus approaches him, pleading that Aeneas arrange for his bones to receive a proper burial so that he may cross the Wailing River and rest in peace. At the climactic moment of Franzen's adventure, after the rigours of weather and landscape have confounded his aspiration to see the extremely rare songbird he's been chasing at some personal risk, and he has nonetheless been rewarded on return to camp with a moment of spectacular beauty, he is finally ready to scatter the ashes.

'At the end of the promontory, I came to a pair of matching boulders that together formed a kind of altar . . . I opened the box of ashes and threw them up into the wind. Some bits of gray bone came down on the slope below me, but the dust was caught in the wind and vanished into the blue vault of the sky, blowing out across the ocean.'

This is as close to the Romantic sublime as Wallace will get, vanishing into infinity on Earth. In what may be the most apt tribute to his friend, however, Franzen acknowledges the impurity of the moment, mixed as it is with his distracting desire to photograph the 'celestial beauty of the landscape' and regret at not having seen the rare bird.

~

streams and into the streets. Above the waterline you pass, a cloud that thinks itself grand but can't yet

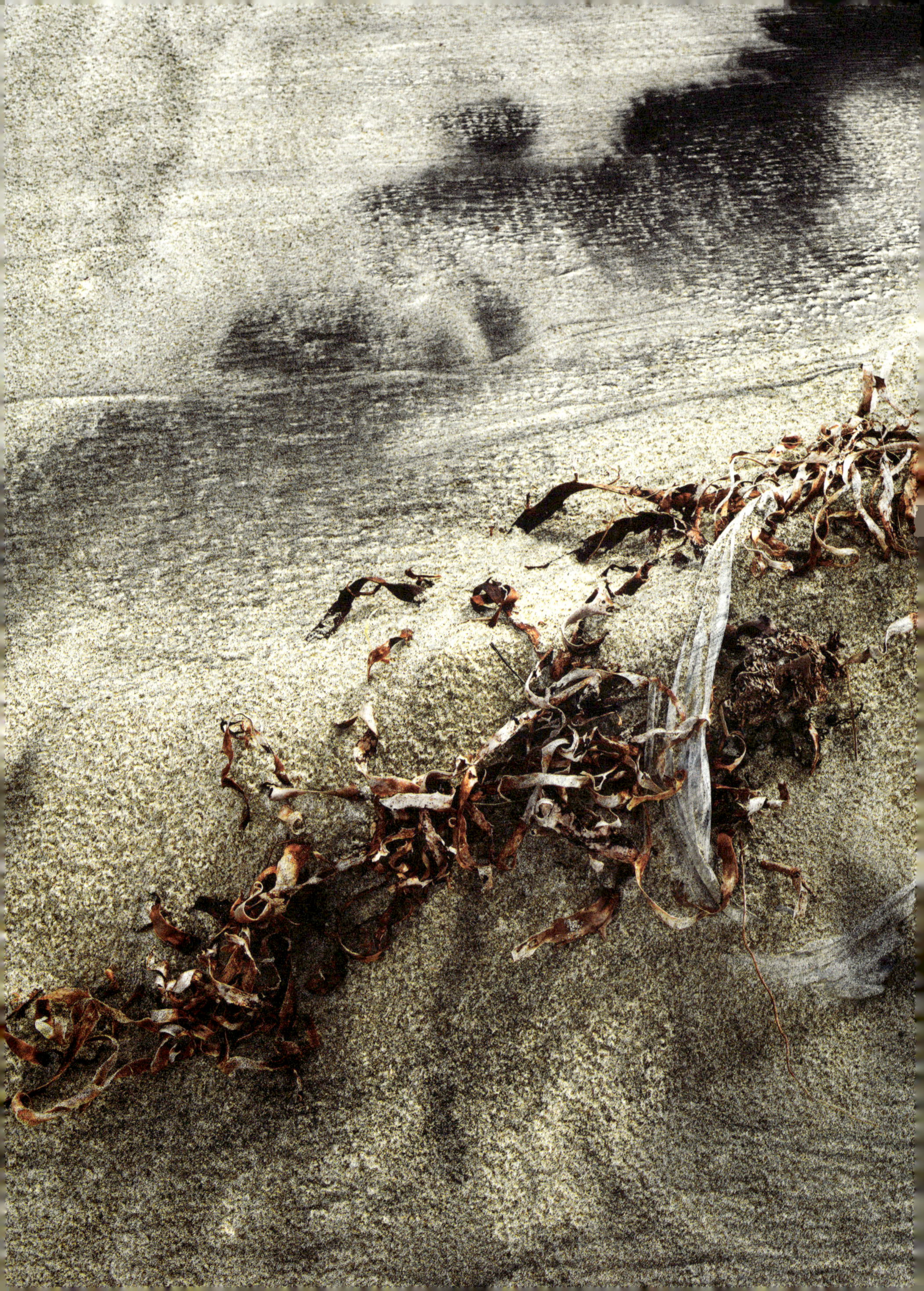

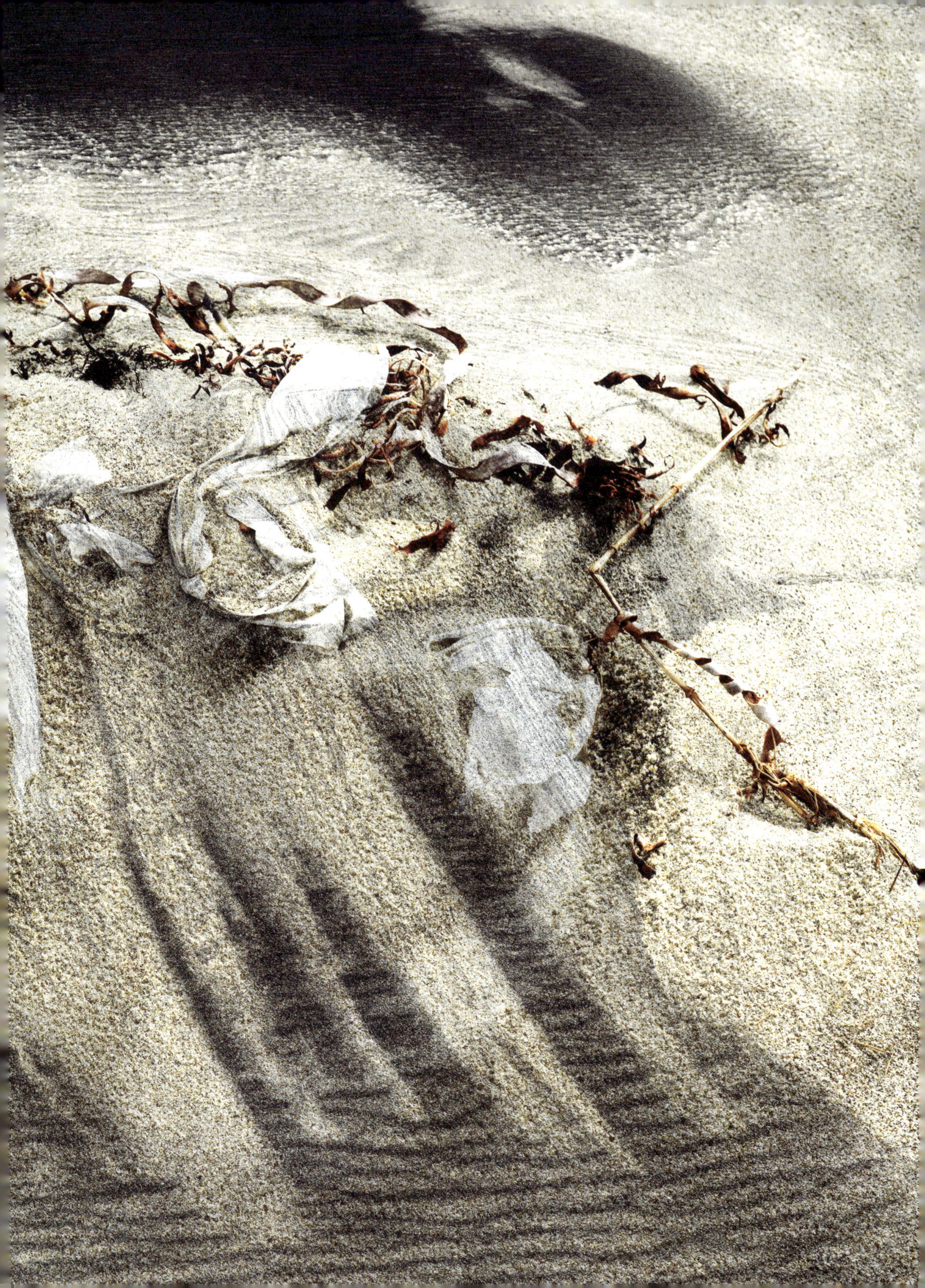

Before his death, Sisyphus instructs his wife to dump his body in the public square instead of giving him a proper burial. In one reading, this is a genuine test of her loyalty; in another, it's a cunning pretext to seek leave from the underworld to revisit his wife and chastise her. Of course, Sisyphus then remains in the sunshine, deaf to the gods' threats and warnings to return below.

Despite the punishing mode of his going (rope, patio), Wallace got the burial love dictates — but not without some anger mixed in. Anger at the damage done to the ones left above ground (the wife whose task it was to find the body and the neat pile of unfinished manuscript, and to dispose appropriately of both). Anger at the abdication of responsibility. Anger at being abandoned without warning. *I don't want him at peace*, writes the wife. It is the living, I think, who must cross the Wailing River.

~

steer a course between malign and beneficent .... It's past time to consider revising the story. Even the

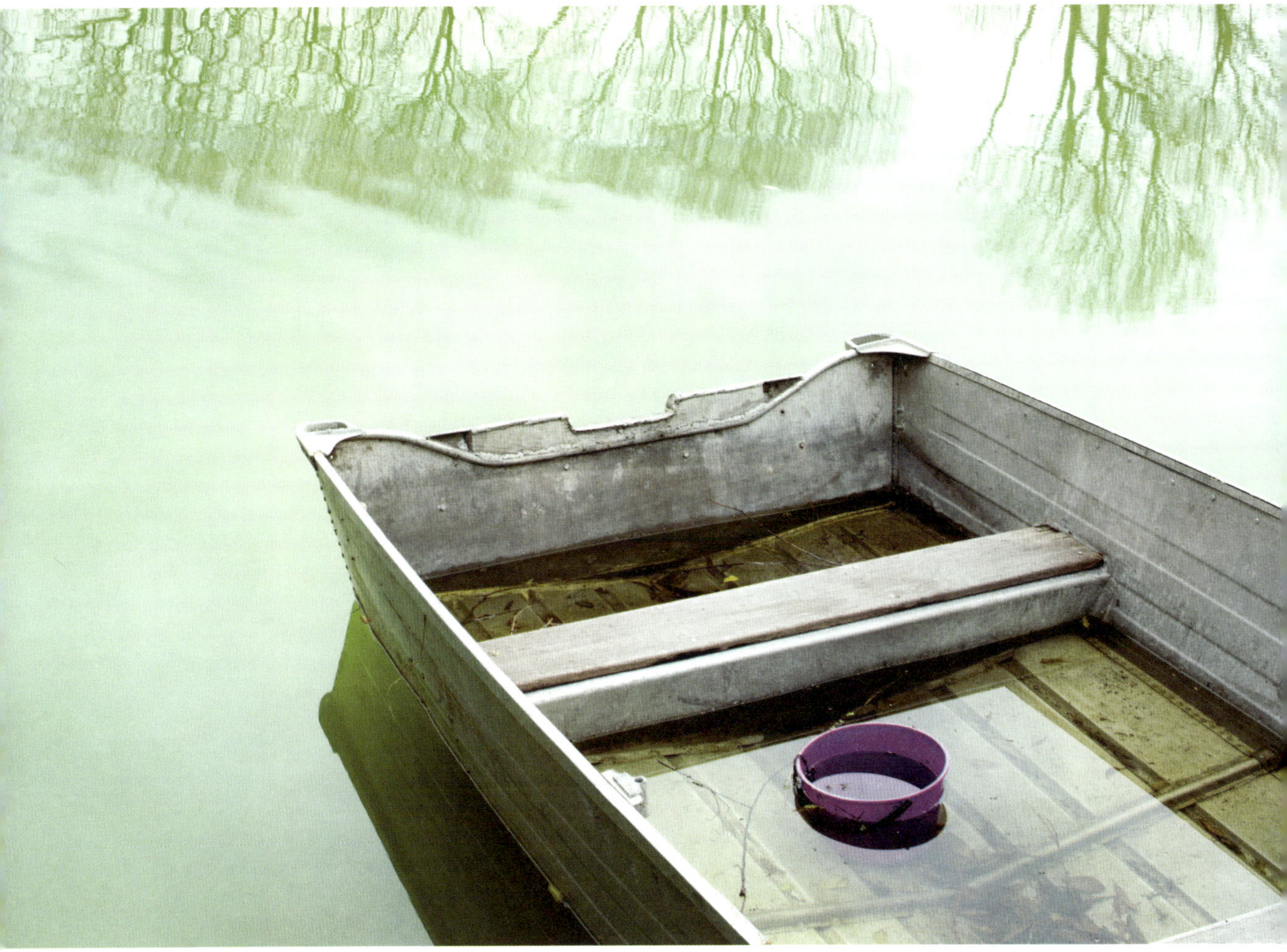

hero needs some open water, not just obstacle, island, iceberg, monster. The hero has worked hard at

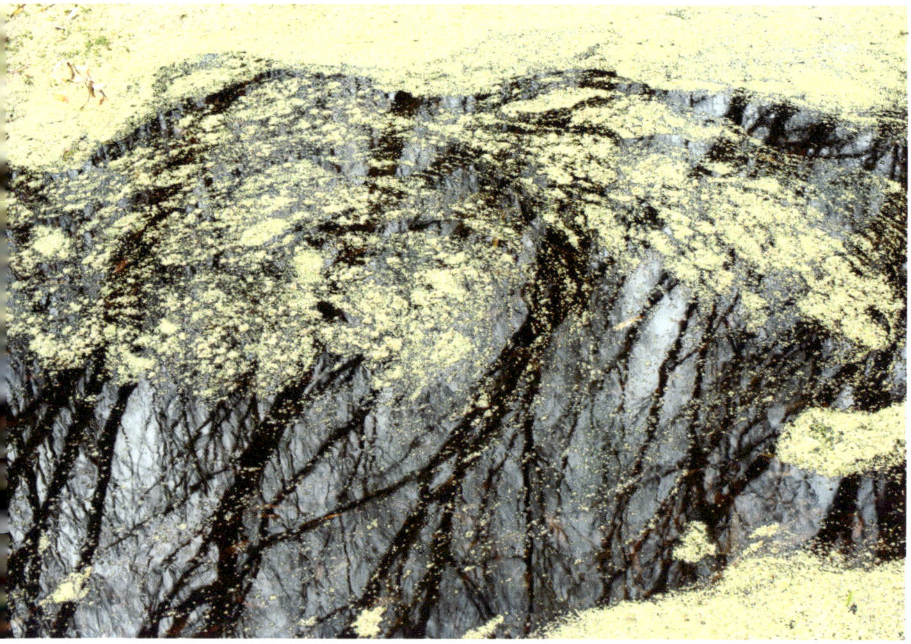 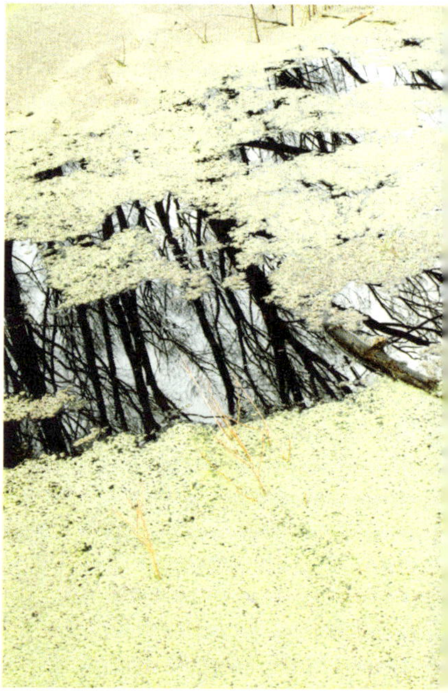

When Franzen has exhausted anger and solitude, he boards the boat back to Selkirk's companion island, Robinson Crusoe (formerly Isla Más a Tierra, the Island Closer to Land), in the company of two skinned goats, an old lobsterman and over a thousand lobsters. But he can't fly back to the Chilean mainland – the cargo plane is so full that even the co-pilot's seat is occupied by cartons of lobster. And so Franzen is temporarily stranded on Robinson Crusoe, but at least he has a book to read: *Robinson Crusoe*.

inscribing his name and tragic flaw upon the ocean; now he needs some quiet time, lullabies, days of

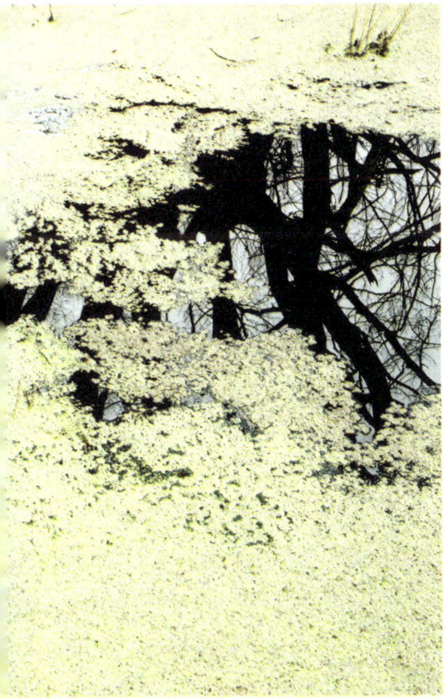
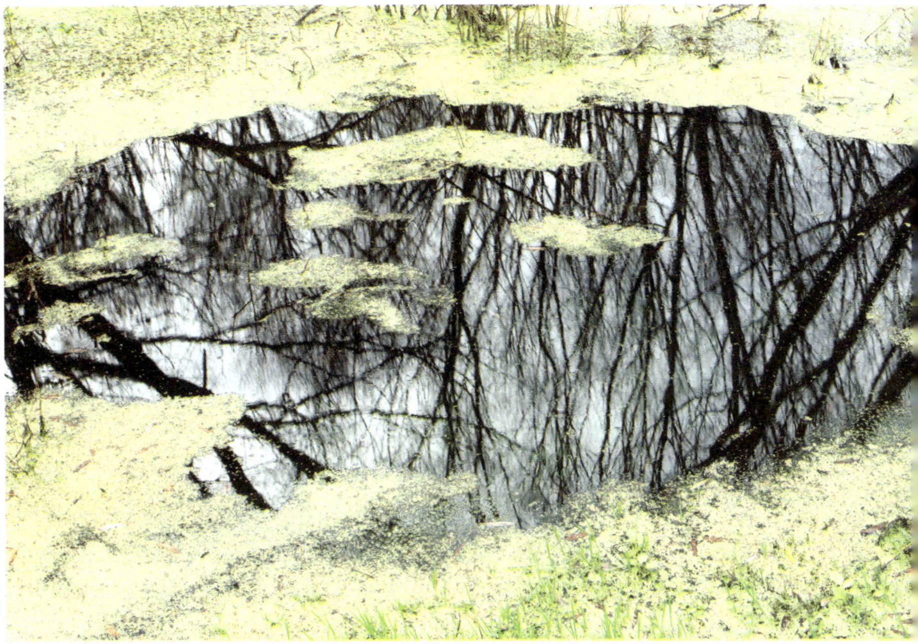

Is an artfully constructed voyage the same as something that 'just happens'? Does anything, for that matter, just happen, or *shall we & / why not* forget such distinctions, and simply acknowledge that all human voyages are impure? Even Camus suggests that 'a man defines himself by his make-believe as well as by his sincere impulses'. Mixed motives, dirty silence: are these not the things that make our make-believe not only possible but necessary?

~

nothing but watching clouds and currents. He needs to settle for a local habitation and a name — so

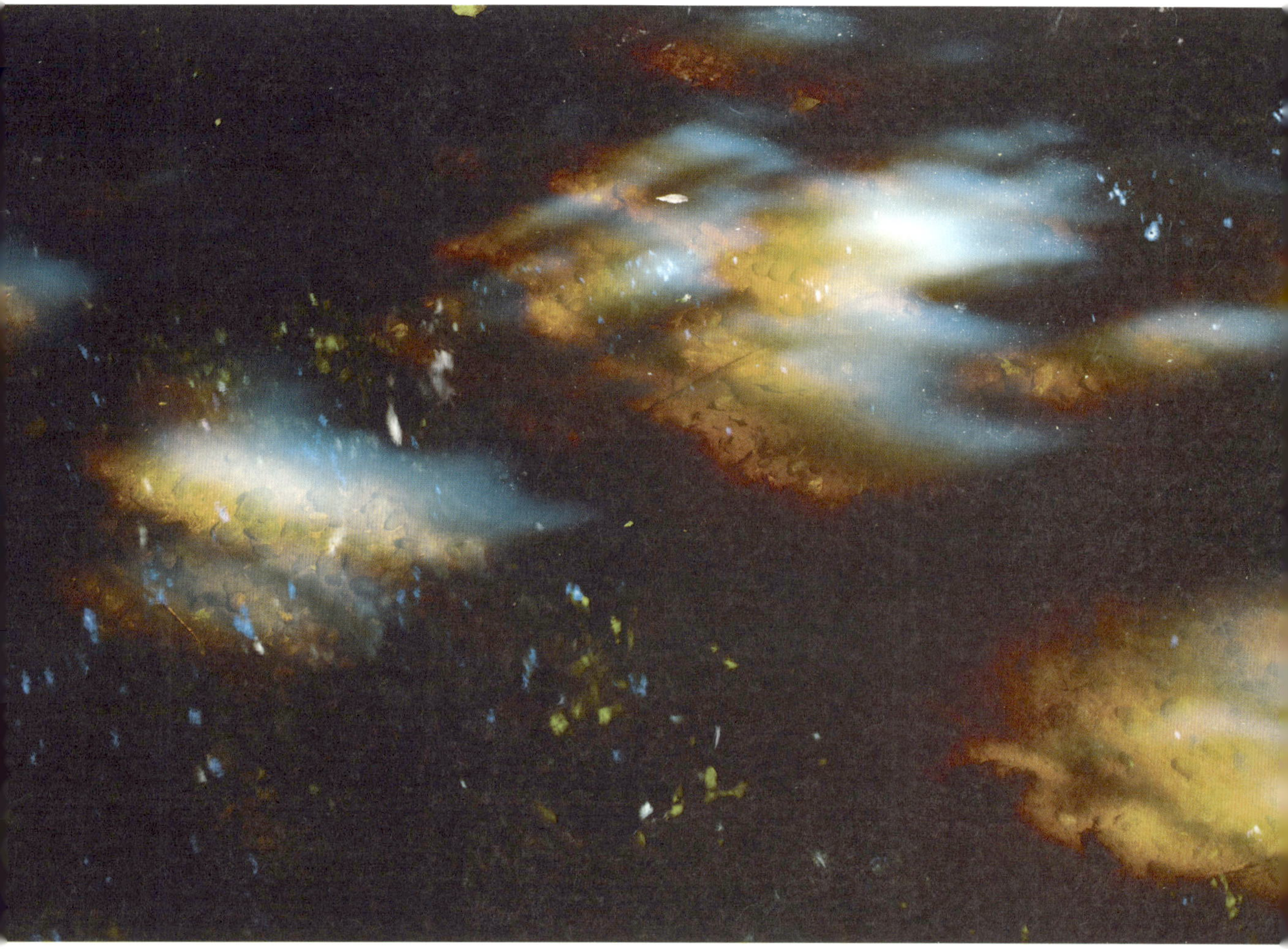

when he comes home from the sea in the evening hour on his ship of death, just try to give him the water

After exploring the coast of Australia, Cook turned for home with Tupaia still on board. The Tahitian navigator and roving ambassador saw the port of Batavia (present-day Jakarta), but he would never see London. He died of scurvy on the island of Kuyper, then in Dutch possession, partway towards England on the longest voyage of his life. Sydney Parkinson records that Tupaia was buried on the island of Edam, now Damar Besar, about eleven thousand kilometres from his home island of Ra'iātea. The jungle has long since covered his grave.

Parkinson too died before he reached home, and was consigned, as they say, to the deep. Tupaia's pet lorikeet, acquired in Australia, made it all the way to the other side of the world, where it lived on in Marmaduke Tunstall's London menagerie.

~

he lacked and went looking for. 'He created an obstacle to conquer, or an enemy to attack; attacked; and

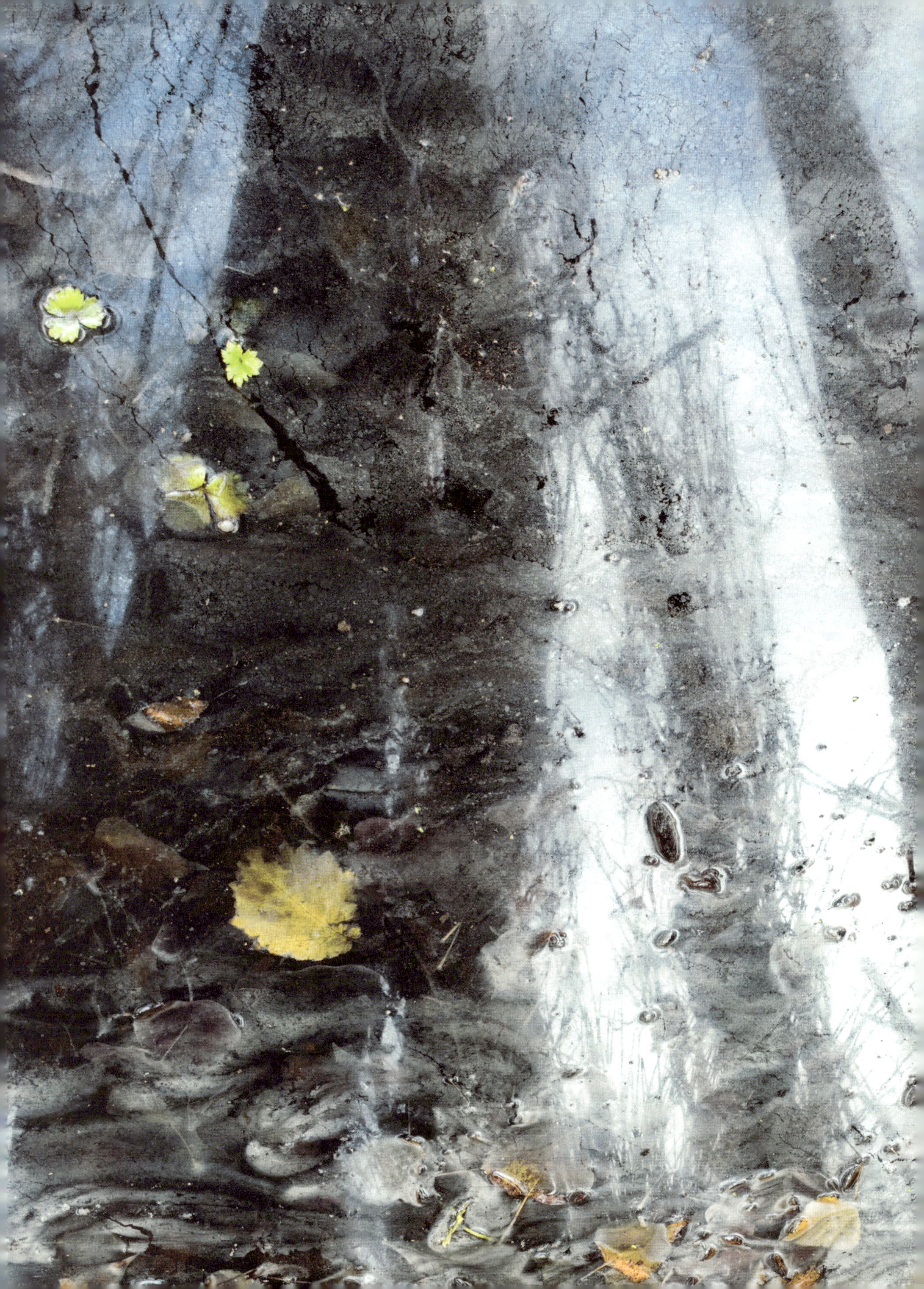

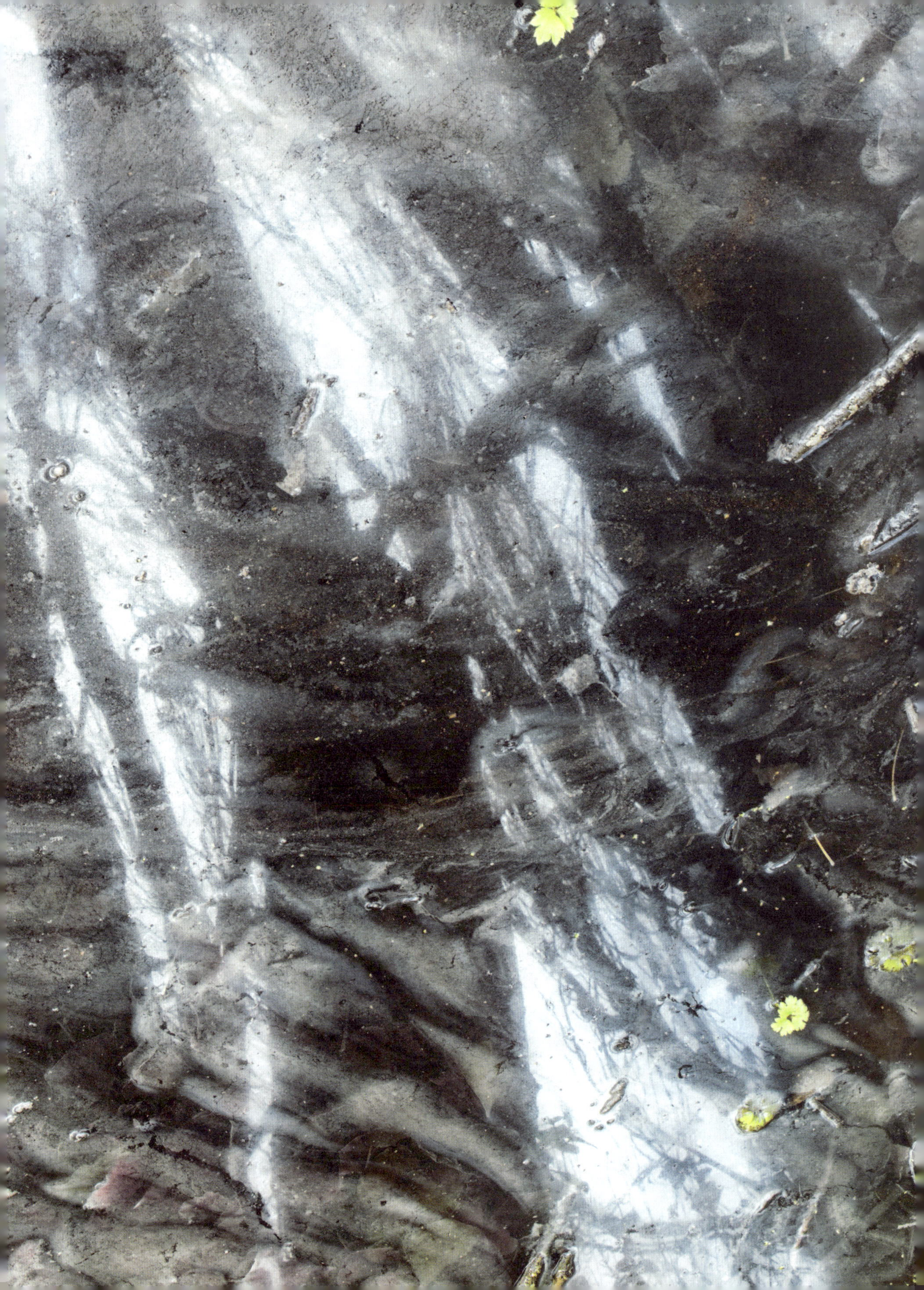

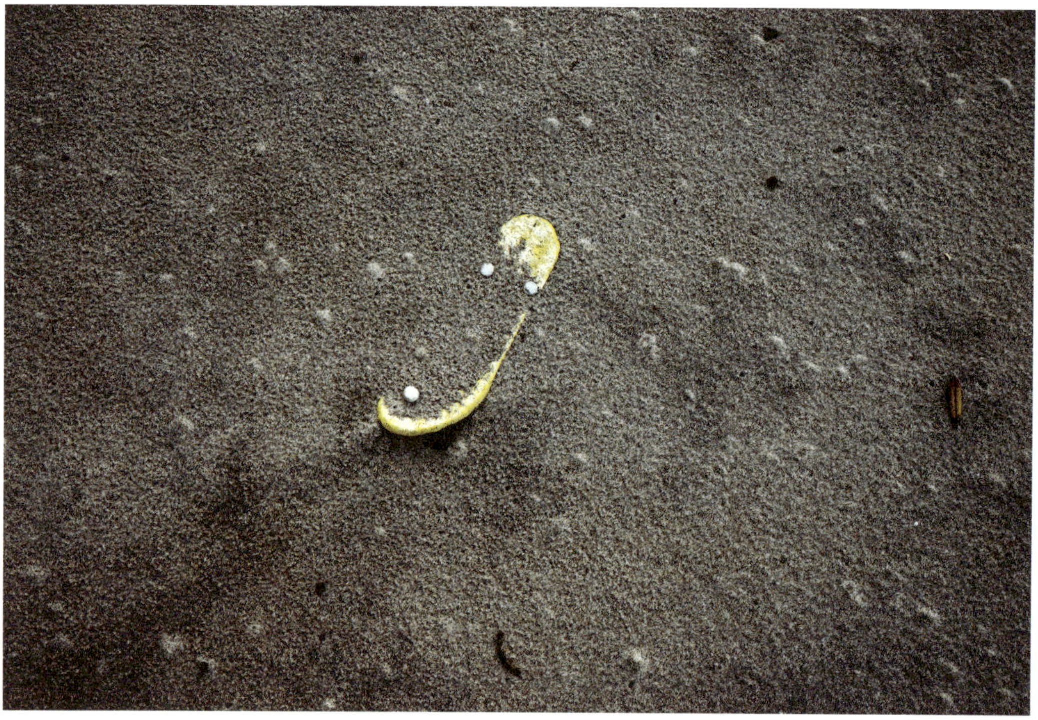

‘At the moment of death,’ writes Camus, ‘the succession of his works is but a collection of failures. But if those failures all have the same resonance, the creator has managed to repeat the image of his own condition, to make the air echo with the sterile secret he possesses.’

~

was defeated — by what? By himself, having himself created the situation in which his defeat could occur.’

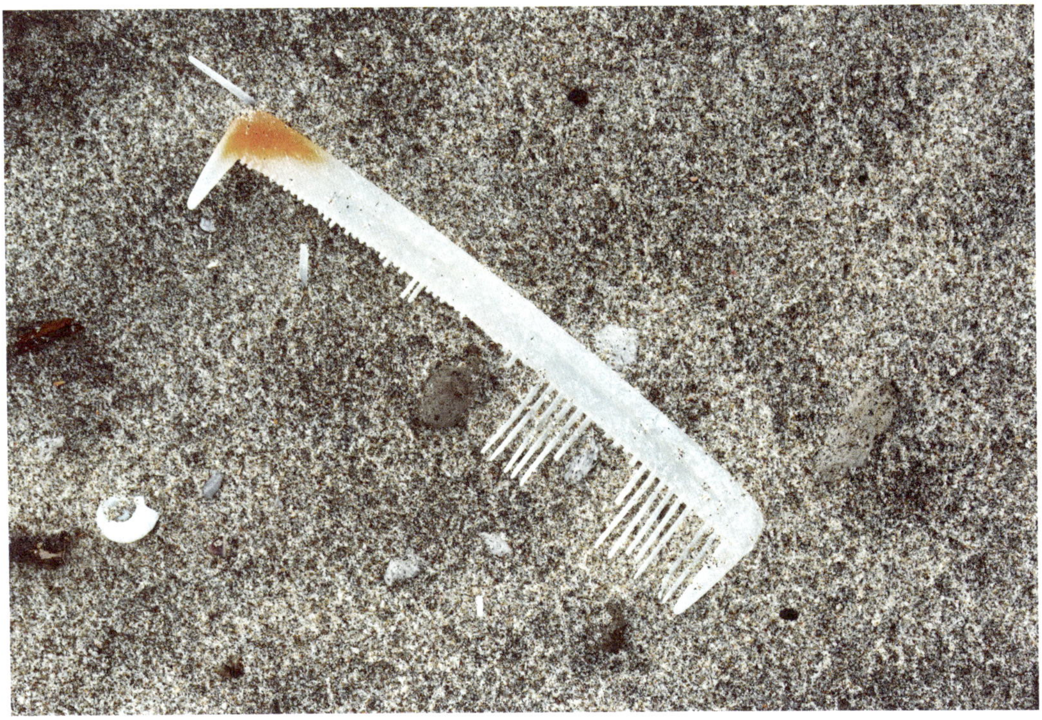

An aspect of human–lobster relations not touched on in Wallace's essay is eyestalk ablation. Apparently, snipping off the lobsters' eyes at the base of the stalk produces much-increased growth. It also leads to lower survival rates, and 'adverse behavioural and colour changes'. Removing just one eyestalk may produce better results.

~

.... Epic time has anyway long since been overtaken by the slow-motion tragedy of a cruise ship headed

Before long, nothing will be invisible, no island remote, no creature unclassified, no thought unspoken (*because I am / always talking*). No *silentes*, only *stridentes*. And yet, as long as they are still available, personal encounters will always have their unique charms and hazards. In 1988 a diver complaining of earache was found to have a puerulus (post-larval-phase lobster) lodged in his ear.

~

for the rocks. Linear time is tunnel vision, but Earth time's a looper, a spiral of recurring consequence.

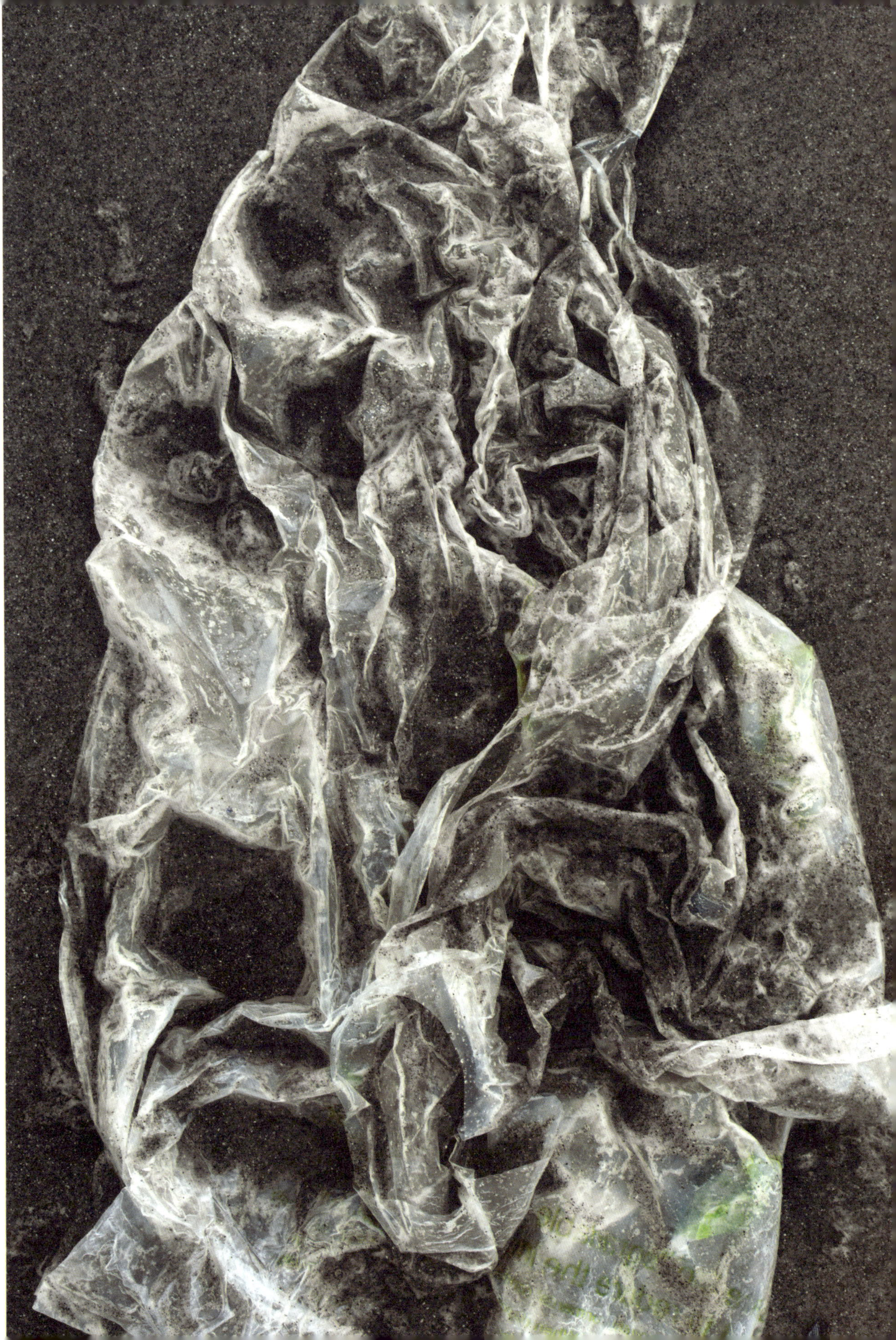

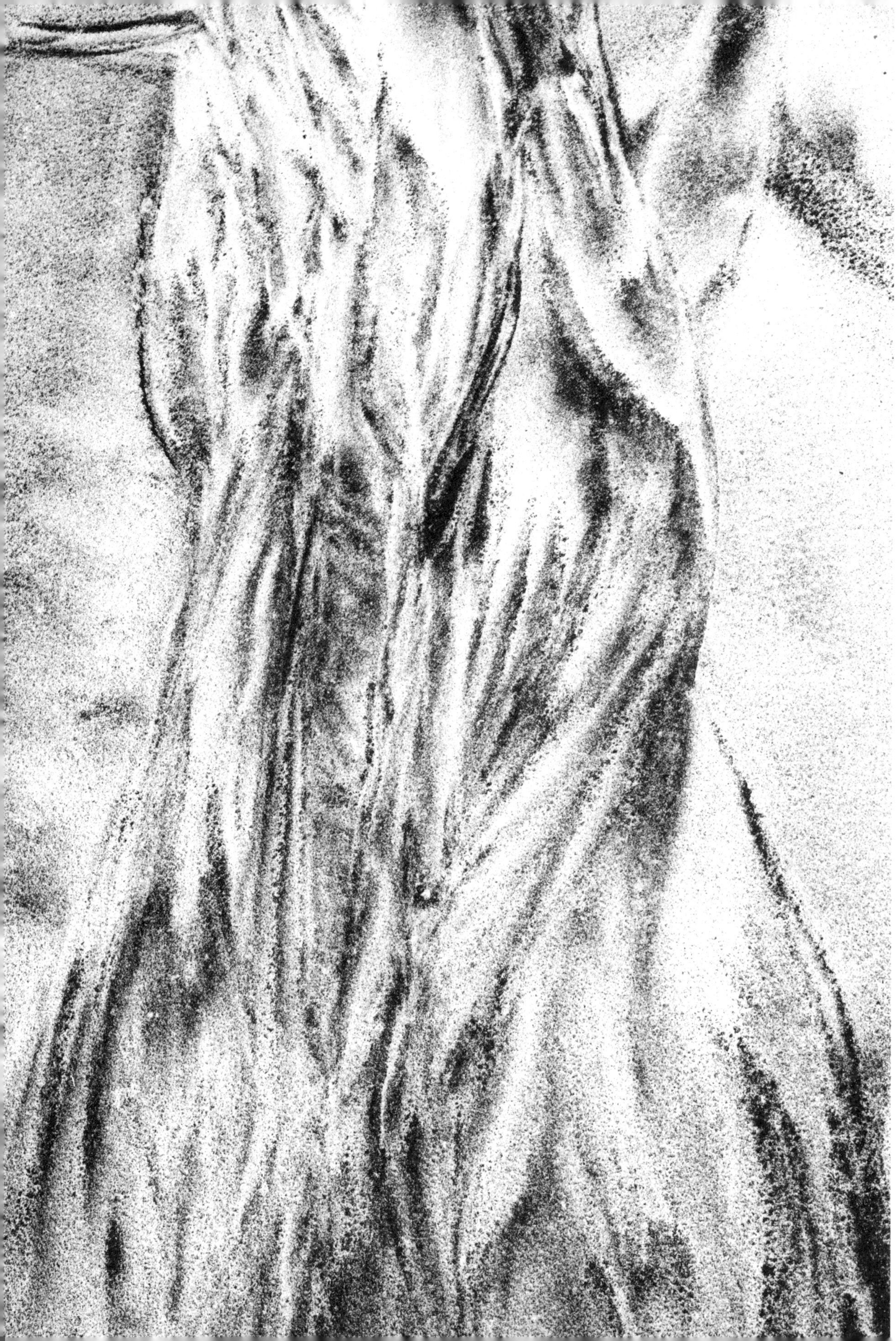

Franzen suggests that 'arguably, in one interpretation of his suicide, David had died of boredom and in despair about his novels'. (For the past decade Wallace had been struggling with the 'novel about boredom' that was published posthumously, in a text assembled by his editor, as *The Pale King*.) 'When his hope for fiction died, after years of struggle with the new novel, there was no other way out but death.'

Not everything, even in the life of a writer, can be accounted for by writing. Still, writers naturally turn to other writers. Wallace was reading Camus shortly before he deserted his post — or was swept overboard.

~

As the ink dries up with the stream and hedge funds trade in water futures, the hero has to live like

In case of emergency, you need a plan to stay connected with those closest to you, and someone to guard your back.

everybody else .... The new courage might be nothing more glamorous than this: to change your fate, suck

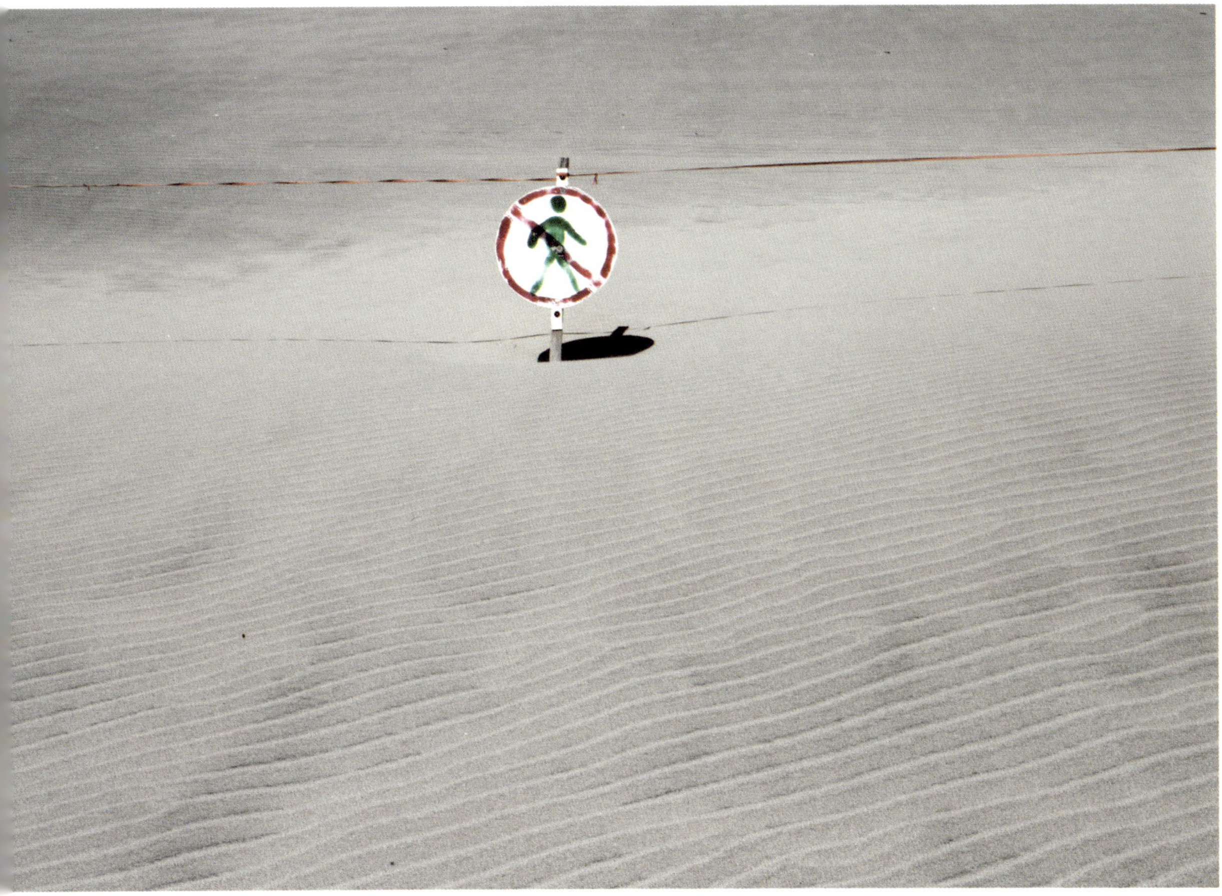

the poison out of the system. The new question: how to be less insidious. As kōura periodically moult,

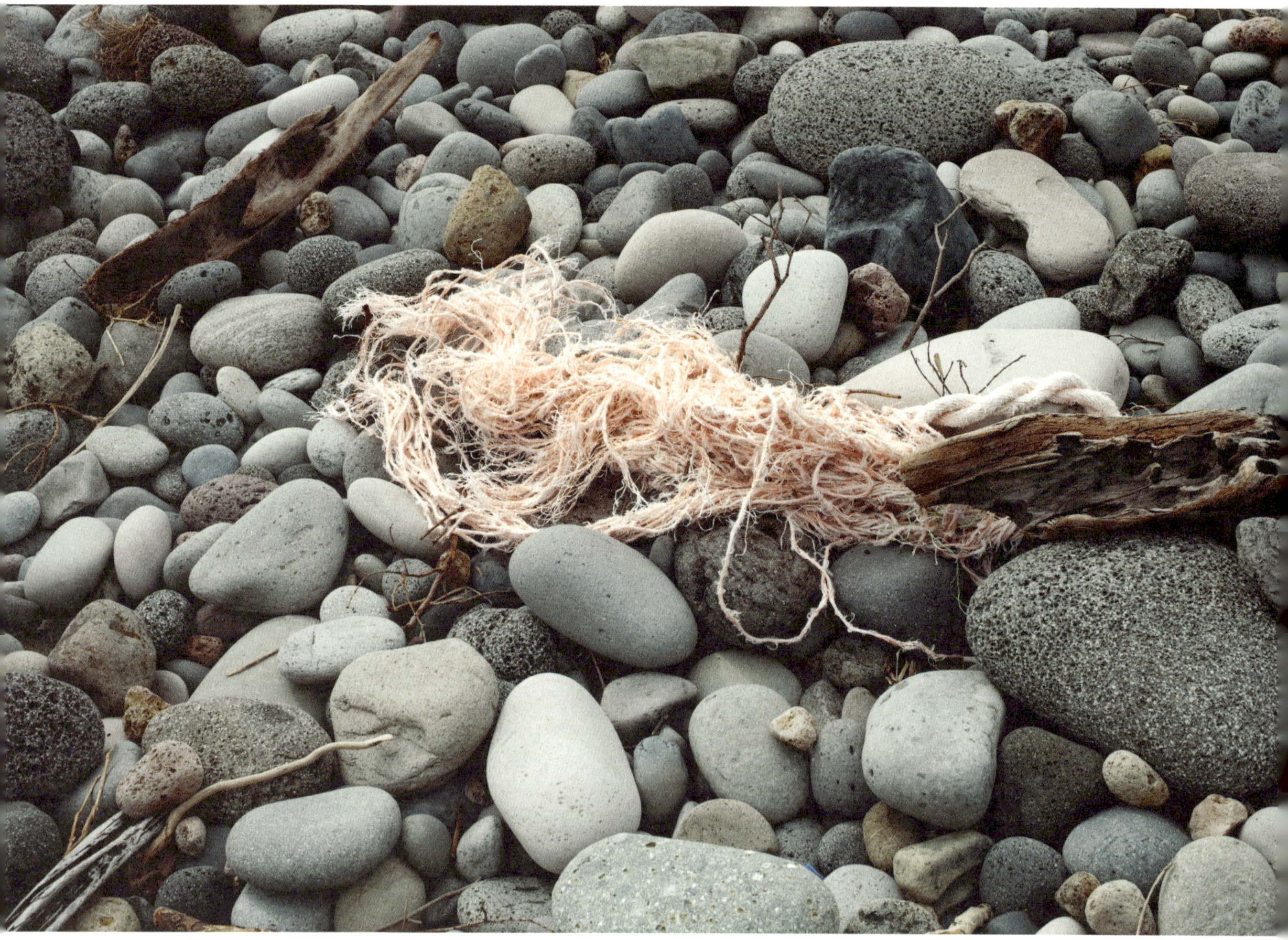

you too might choose the necessity your disintegrating story forces on you and jump ship from its ever-

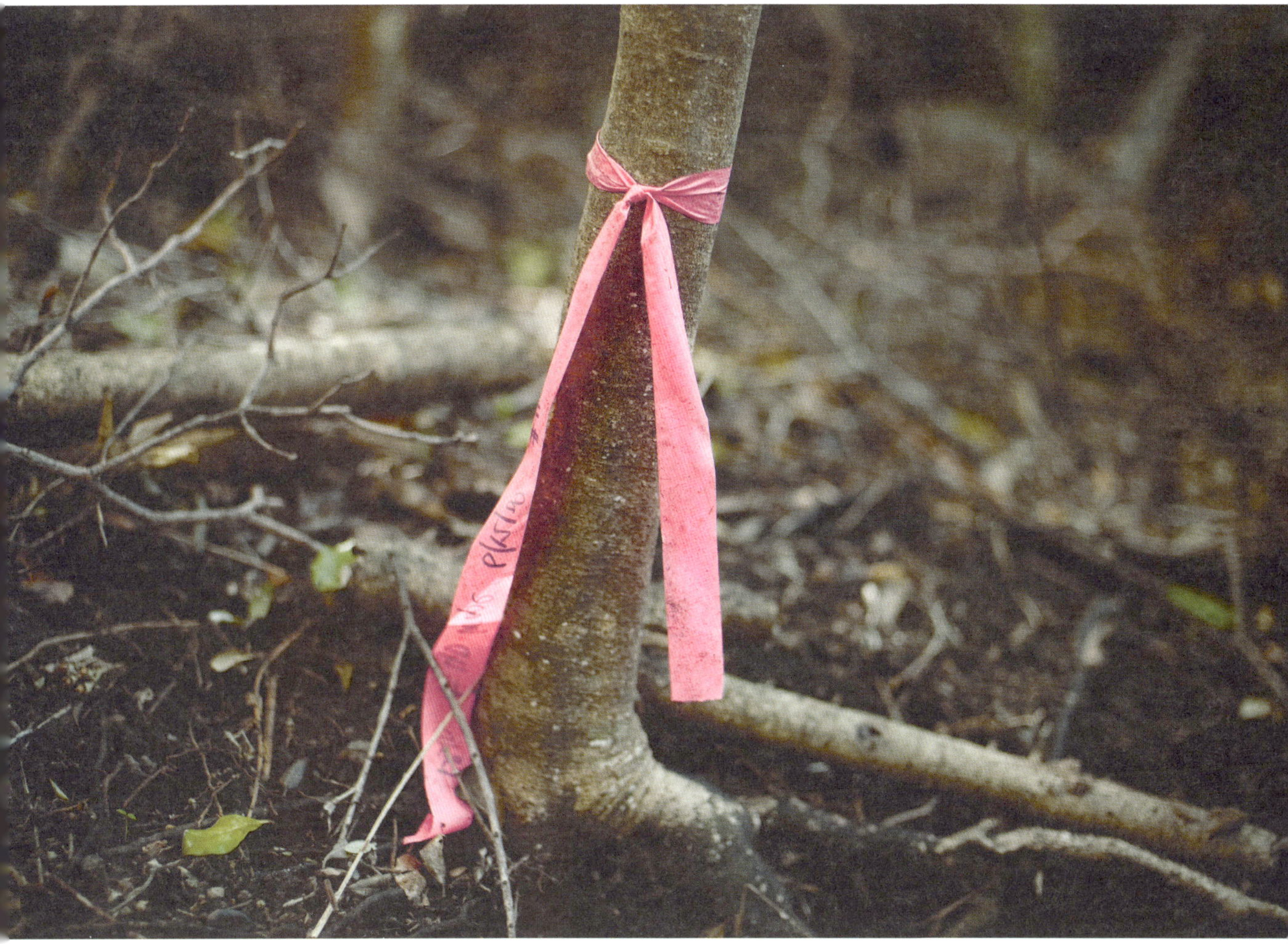

tightening constraints. The strength of navigators might now be kybernetikos, a gift for working deftly

At the ends of our chromosomes are DNA sequences called telomeres, which protect them in much the way plastic tips protect the ends of shoelaces, preventing them from fraying and sticking together, and enabling cells to divide. Telomere shortening is a key factor in the genetic deterioration that causes ageing. In *Homarus americanus*, the enzyme telomerase is switched on in every cell, so the lobsters have no telomere shortening. They continue to grow and reproduce throughout their lives, and show no discernible signs of ageing. We have no idea, say the scientists, how long these lobsters might live if they did not succumb to disease or predation. Some of these scientists are exploring the potential routes to immortality.

On the other hand, cancer cells also achieve longevity by circumventing the process of telomere shortening. And it is unlikely that Thibault walked far or survived long in Paris — unless his poet sought advice from Milne Edwards on how to keep him. Nerval chose to take the same exit as Wallace, as it happens, at about the same age, and for similar reasons.

~

with the governing mechanisms of a system in which cause and effect can't be readily distinguished ....

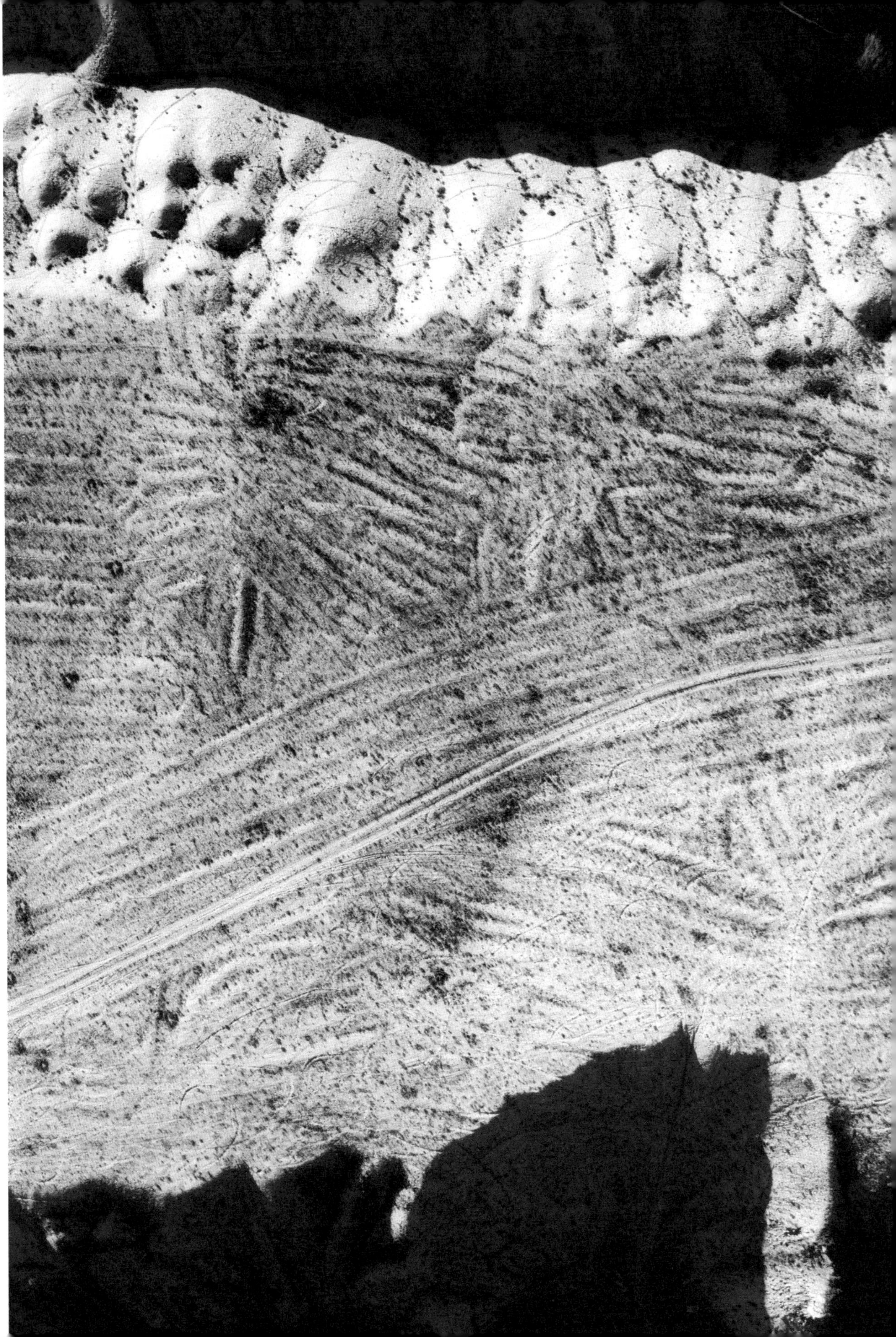

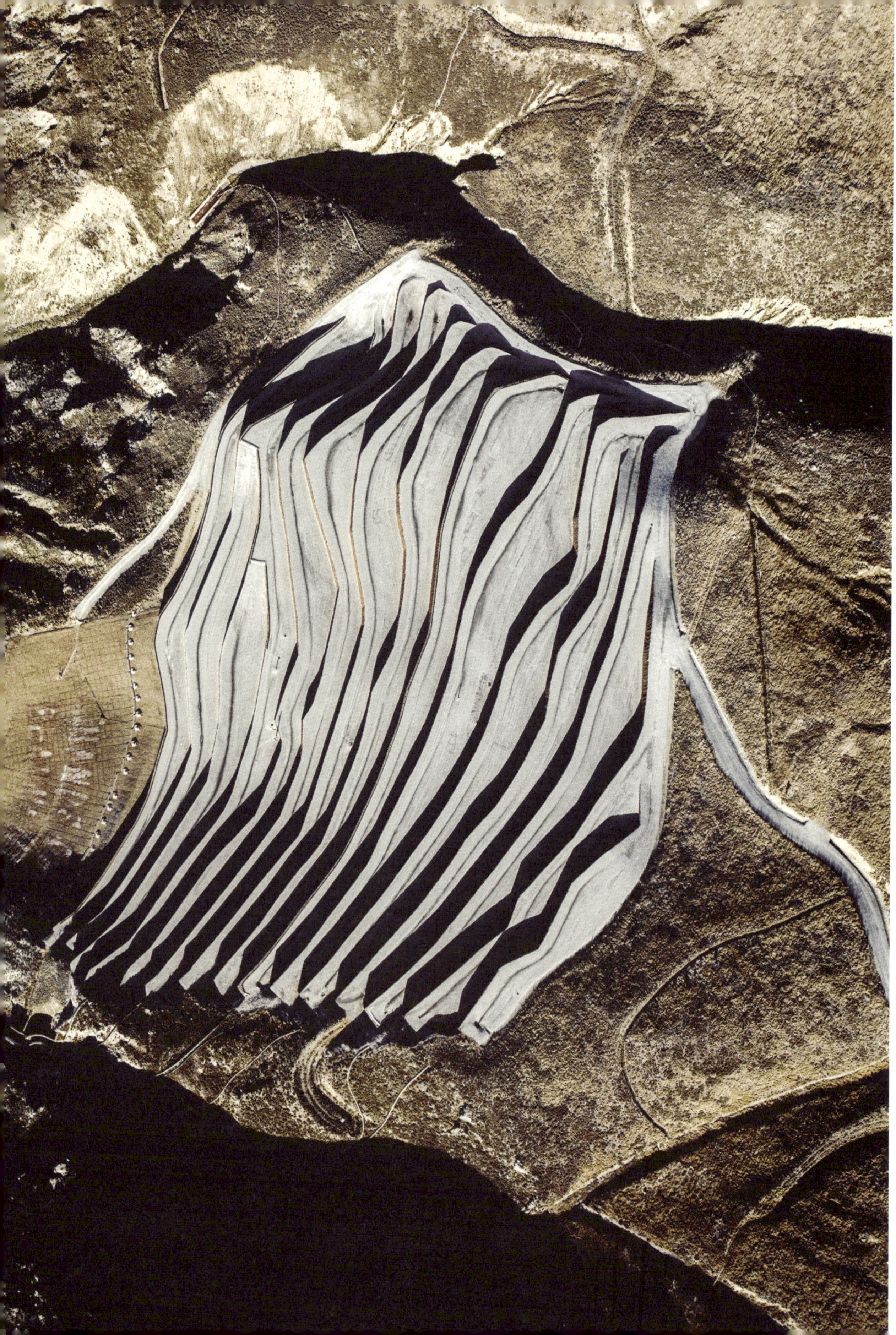

In 2013, global warming — or so it was thought — produced a lobster glut in America, yet despite the resulting drop in price, lobster remained a high-cost item in restaurants. *New Yorker* writer James Surowiecki suggested this was because lobster is less a commodity than a luxury good — in other words, price is determined by perception as much as availability. If it's cheap on today's menu, how can restaurateurs sell it at a premium tomorrow, when supply decreases and the price goes up again? Plus, an expensive lobster thermidor makes other menu items look more reasonable. When it comes to lobster, said Surowiecki, price setting is a 'surprisingly complex attempt to both respond to and shape what customers want'. In this it resembles the art market and the wine market, those Elysian fields governed by the arcane values that pertain when one reaches the tip of the pyramid of human needs. For *New Yorker* readers, the world remains available to be consumed.

~

Look to the life that goes on in your blind spot, the light that will eat you alive. Ahead remains a narrowing

In Madagascar, the marbled crayfish (or *foza orana*, as the locals call her) now enjoys the status of perfect invader. Bypassing the more common laws of reproduction and evolution, she is the only member of her ancient family that is parthenogenetic, and thus a rampant threat to the island's endemic species. In this strange time when even lobsters can fly, she flew from Louisiana to Frankfurt in the baggage of exotic pet dealers, perhaps acquiring her parthenogenetic mutation in the extreme cold of the cargo hold. Cultivated in a German aquarium, she travelled to Madagascar, where her burrows undermine the rice paddies and she eats the larvae of more valuable species but also feeds the poor. 'In Malagasy slang,' writes Rowan Moore Gerety, '*foza orana* has become a kind of insult, shorthand for anything that is abundant, cheap, and low quality.' Both pest and protein, the marbled crayfish is an unnatural resource. There has always been more to care about than most of us have cared to know.

~

gap no creature can thread solo, by exercise of will or control, but only in collaboration: you might

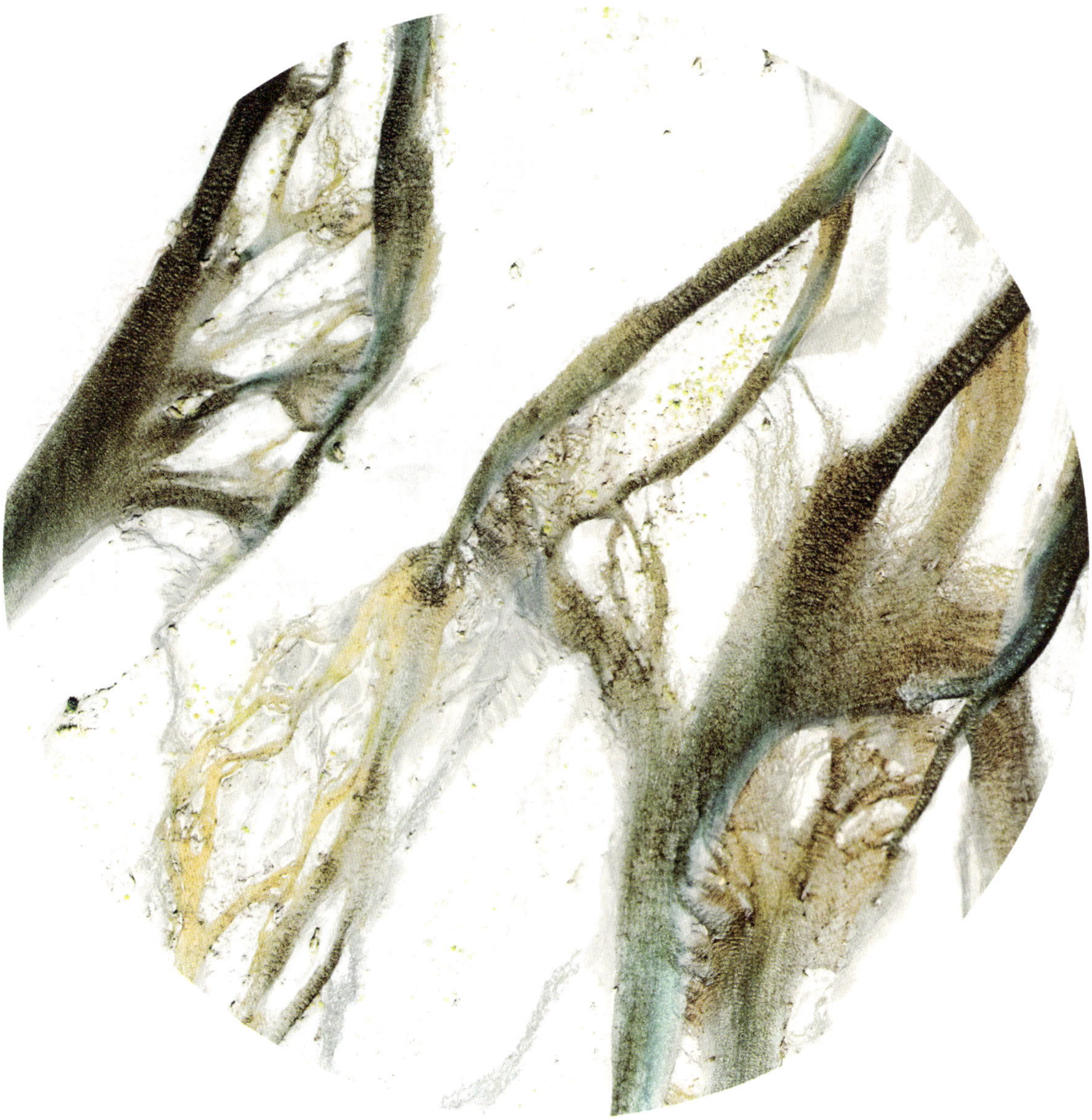

choose to carry each other as the kōura in berry carries eggs below her tail until they're fit to burst, then

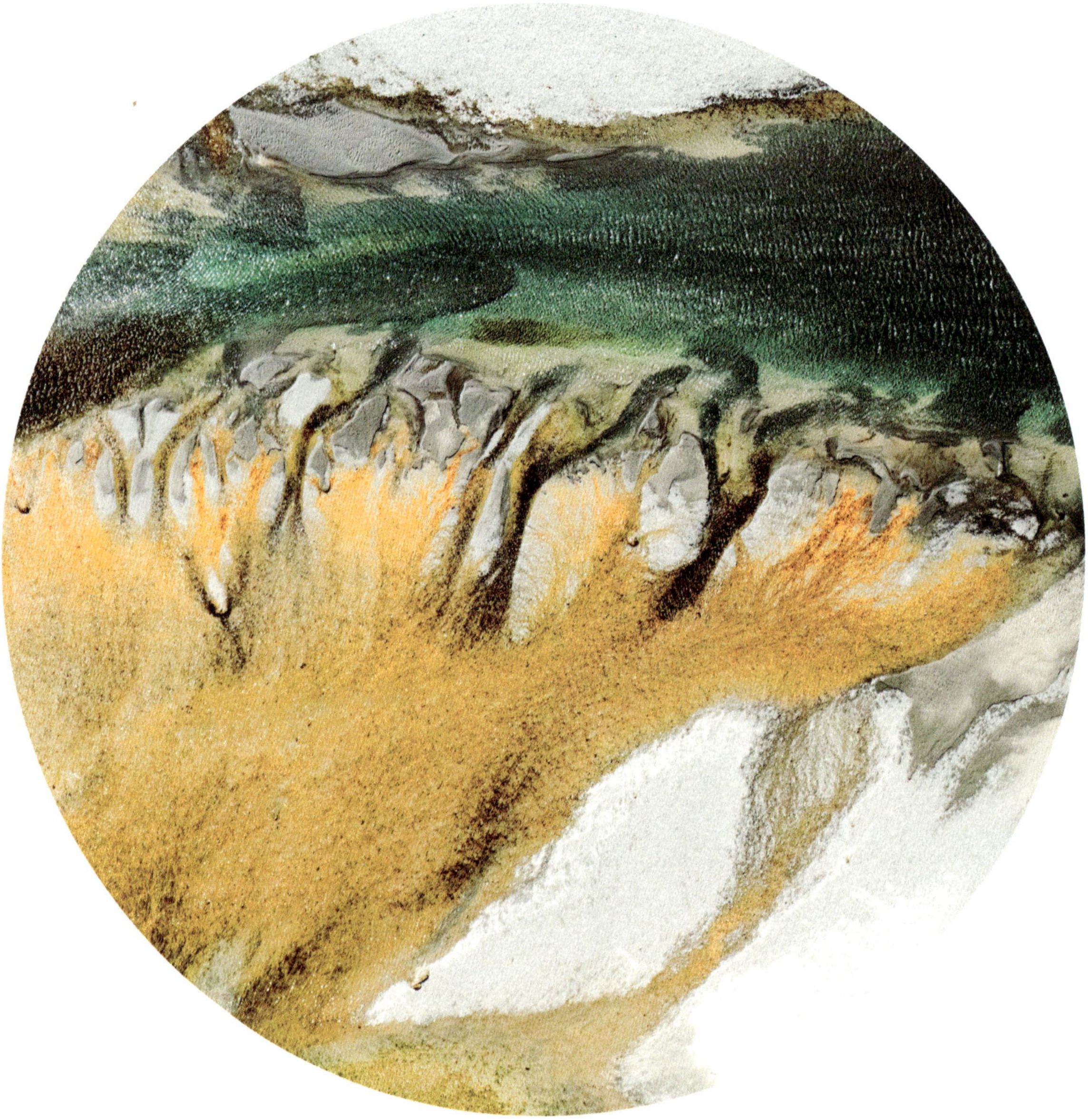

carries her offspring a few weeks more until they're ready to let go. You too are water — but the old gods

'The absurd man says yes and his effort will henceforth be unceasing. If there is a personal fate, there is no higher destiny, or at least there is but one, which he concludes is inevitable and despicable.' Arguably, in one interpretation of *The Pale King*, Wallace was trying to find his own way of saying yes to the meaningless labours of Sisyphus, to the absurdity of existence. 'For the rest, he knows himself to be the master of his days. Sisyphus returning toward his rock, in that slight pivoting he contemplates that series of unrelated actions which becomes his fate, created by him, combined under his memory's eye and soon sealed by his death. Thus, convinced of the wholly human origin of all that is human, a blind man eager to see who knows that the night has no end, he is still on the go. The rock is still rolling.'

Out of clear-eyed and level-headed despair, divested of the false consolations offered by God or the gods, Camus answers Hamlet's question in the affirmative. The last sentence of *The Myth of Sisyphus*: 'The struggle towards the heights is enough to fill a man's heart. One must imagine Sisyphus happy.'

~

don't need the irrigation of your praise or tears; they need your aid, your patient, repetitive devotions.

Having justified the choice of existence over self-annihilation, Camus died in a car crash.

They need your mouth-to-mouth resuscitation . . .

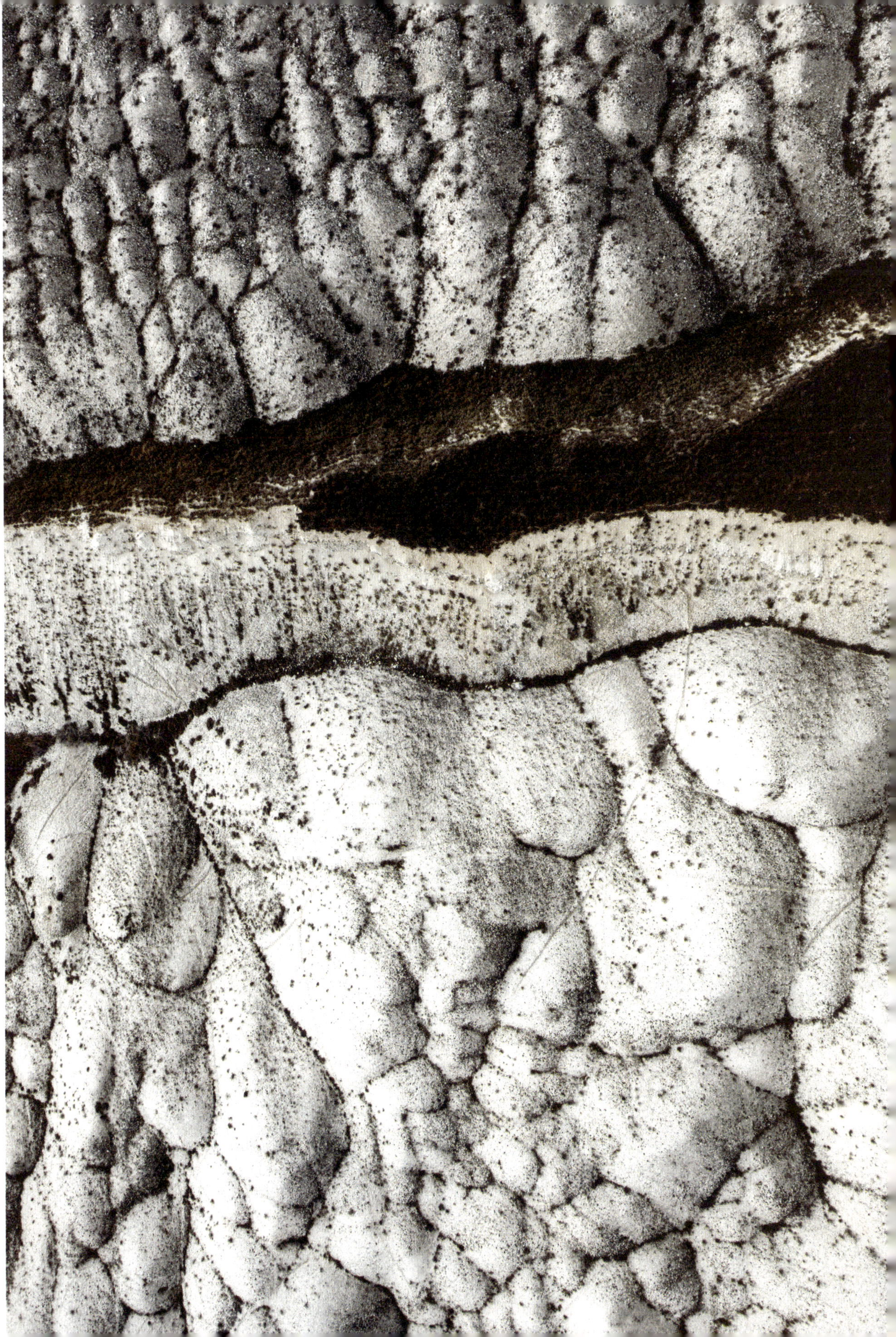

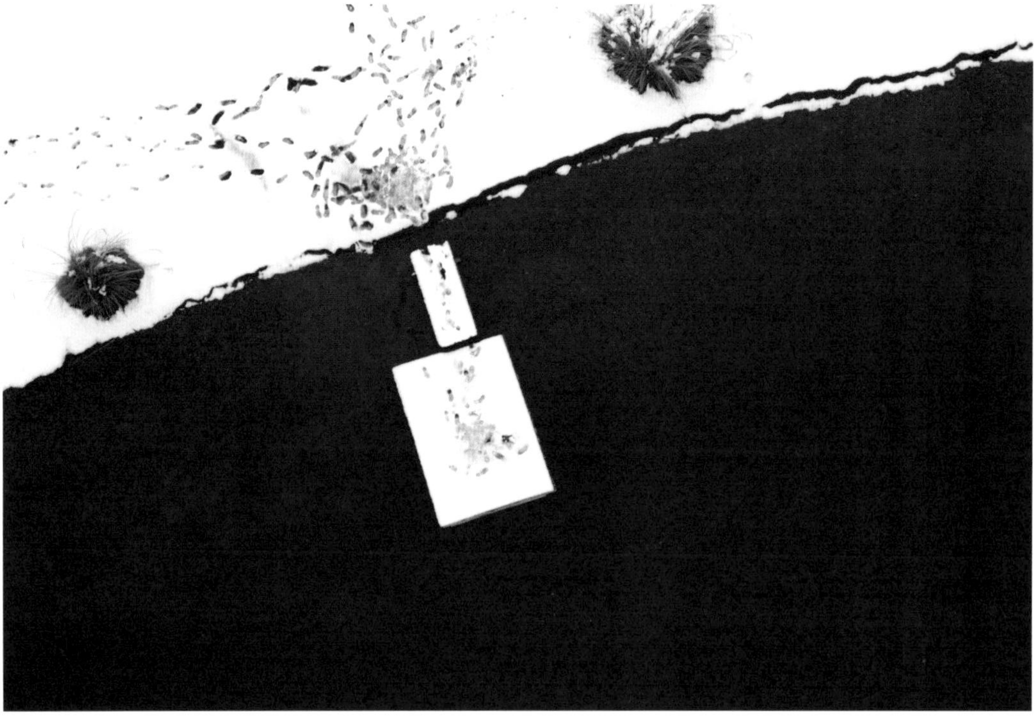

It is unlikely that Selkirk ever set foot on the island that now bears his name.

Notes

Much of the information on lobster biology and ecology in this book is drawn from Bruce Phillips (ed.), *Lobsters: Biology, Management, Aquaculture and Fisheries* (Oxford: Blackwell, 2006), and John Booth, *Spiny Lobsters: Through the Eyes of the Giant Packhorse* (Wellington: Victoria University Press, 2011). Additional information on kōura comes from the websites of NIWA and Zealandia. The two lobsters illustrated on the endpapers of this book are the European or common lobster *Homarus gammarus* (front) and the New Zealand freshwater crayfish or kōura *Paranephrops planifrons* (back).

p. 3 '*What is the lobster's tune . . .*': Thomas Lovell Beddoes, 'Death's Jest-Book', in H. W. Donner (ed.), *The Works of Thomas Lovell Beddoes* (London: Oxford University Press, 1935).

p. 6 Gérard de Nerval's thoughts on lobsters were recorded by Théophile Gautier in *Portraits et souvenirs littéraires* (Charpentier, 1875), trans. Richard Holmes, *My Fantoms* (London: Quartet, 1976).

p. 9 '*there's much more to know . . .*': David Foster Wallace, *Consider the Lobster* (New York: Little, Brown, 2005).

p. 13 '*A profound thought . . .*': Albert Camus, *The Myth of Sisyphus and Other Essays*, trans. Justin O'Brien (New York: Vintage, 1991).

p. 14 '*In the bathysphere . . .*': This below-the-waterline 'paragraph' contains material adapted from William Beebe, *Half Mile Down* (London: John Lane, The Bodley Head, 1935).

p. 15 '*Death, thou shalt die*': John Donne, Holy Sonnet X ('Death be not proud'), in Roy Booth (ed.), *The Collected Poems of John Donne* (Ware: Wordsworth Editions, 2002).

p. 15 An account of Tupaia's voyage is told in Joan Druett, *Tupaia: The Remarkable Story of Captain Cook's Polynesian Navigator* (Auckland: Random House, 2011).

p. 15 'Palinuridae, *the clawless family of spiny lobsters that play the violin . . .*': Adam Summers, 'The Lobster's Violin', http://faculty.washington.edu/fishguy/Articles/Lobsters-Violin.html

p. 16 '*the darkness sur- / rounds us*', '*shall we & / why not*' and '*because I am / always talking*': Robert Creeley, 'I know a man', *Selected Poems* (Berkeley: University of California Press, 1991). Permission courtesy University of California Press.

p. 23 *'Nay he upon societies . . .'*: John Wolcot ('Peter Pindar'), 'Sir Joseph Banks and the Boiled Fleas', *The Works of Peter Pindar*, vol. 2 (London: Walker & Edwards, 1816).

p. 33 *'he did not hesitate to risk his life'*: 'Henri Milne Edwards', *Geological Magazine* 2, no. 10 (Cambridge: Cambridge University Press, 1885), doi:10.1017/S0016756800152690.

p. 36 *'Ancestor, my old incarnation . . .'*: Cyril Connolly, *The Unquiet Grave* (London: Horizon, 1944).

p. 41 *'Foundation Seamounts rock lobster . . .'*: From a table in Booth, *Spiny Lobsters*.

p. 53 *'adventurous botanists'*: Jonathan Franzen, 'Farther Away: "Robinson Crusoe", David Foster Wallace, and the Island of Solitude', *New Yorker*, 18 April 2011.

p. 53 *'In Selkirk's day, or so Diana Souhami claims . . .'*: Diana Souhami, *Selkirk's Island* (London: Weidenfeld & Nicolson, 2001).

p. 62 *'I don't want him at peace'*: Karen Green, *Bough Down* (Los Angeles: Siglio Press, 2013).

p. 65 *'dirty silence'*: Bill Manhire, 'Dirty Silence: Impure Sounds in New Zealand Poetry', in Graham McGregor, Mark Williams and Ray Harlow (eds), *Dirty Silence: Aspects of Language and Literature in New Zealand* (Auckland: Oxford University Press, 1991).

p. 67 *'He created an obstacle to conquer . . .'*: This below-the-waterline quotation is from Ursula K. Le Guin, 'Heroes', in *Dancing at the Edge of the World* (Boulder, CO: Paladin Press, 1992).

p. 71 *'adverse behavioural and colour changes'*: Booth, *Spiny Lobsters*.

p. 83 *'surprisingly complex attempt . . .'*: James Surowiecki, 'Clawback', *New Yorker*, 26 August 2013.

p. 84 *'perfect invader'*: 'The Perfect Invader' is the title of a 2008 paper on the marbled lobster by Jeanne Rasamy and Julia Jones, cited by Rowan Moore Gerety in 'Stowaways', *Harper's Magazine*, February 2021; *'unnatural resources'* is Gerety's phrase.

About the contributors

Chris Price's work often hovers around the intersections between literature and science. She is the author of three poetry collections, *Husk* (Best First Book of Poetry, Montana NZ Book Awards, 2002), *The Blind Singer* (2009) and *Beside Herself* (2016), as well as the hybrid 'biographical dictionary' *Brief Lives* (shortlisted, Montana NZ Book Awards' biography category, 2007). Chris is a former editor of the literary journal *Landfall*. Since 2009 she has convened the MA workshop in poetry and creative nonfiction at the International Institute of Modern Letters, Victoria University of Wellington.

Bruce Foster's current photographs consider the impacts on nature of political decisions and corporate actions. Recent touring exhibitions that include his work are: 'Kermadec Project: Lines Across the Ocean', an initiative articulating the issues facing one of the few pristine ocean sites left on the planet; 'Wai, the Water Project', an exploration of the cultural, conceptual and imaginative aspects of waterways and the existential threats they face; and 'Toitū Te Whenua — The Land Will Always Remain'. The photographs in this book were made between 1996 and 2020. For more information visit brucefoster.nz.

Gary Stewart is an Otago-based designer (The Gas Project), who is well known and highly regarded for his work in book publishing. He is the designer of all the books in the kōrero series.

Acknowledgements

We are grateful to Lloyd Jones for commissioning the earlier version of *The Lobster's Tale* that appeared in the *Griffith Review*, and for the creative matchmaking that brought us together to reinvent it in book form. Thanks also to Gary Stewart and the team at Massey University Press for their willingness to go the extra mile: 'onwards, backwards, sideways, onwards!'

The Lobster's Tale is the third book in the kōrero series. The kōrero project invites new and exciting collaborations for two different kinds of artistic intelligence to work away at a shared topic. Other books in the series are *High Wire*, by Lloyd Jones and Euan Macleod, and *Shining Land*, by Paula Morris and Haru Sameshima.

MASSEY UNIVERSITY PRESS

First published in 2021 by Massey University Press
Private Bag 102904, North Shore Mail Centre
Auckland 0745, New Zealand
www.masseypress.ac.nz

Design by Bruce Foster and Gary Stewart, The Gas Project
Cover photographs by Bruce Foster

A catalogue record for this book is available from the National Library of New Zealand

The assistance of Creative New Zealand is gratefully acknowledged by the publisher

creative nz
ARTS COUNCIL OF NEW ZEALAND TOI AOTEAROA

Printed and bound in China by Everbest Investment Ltd

ISBN: 978-0-9951378-1-3

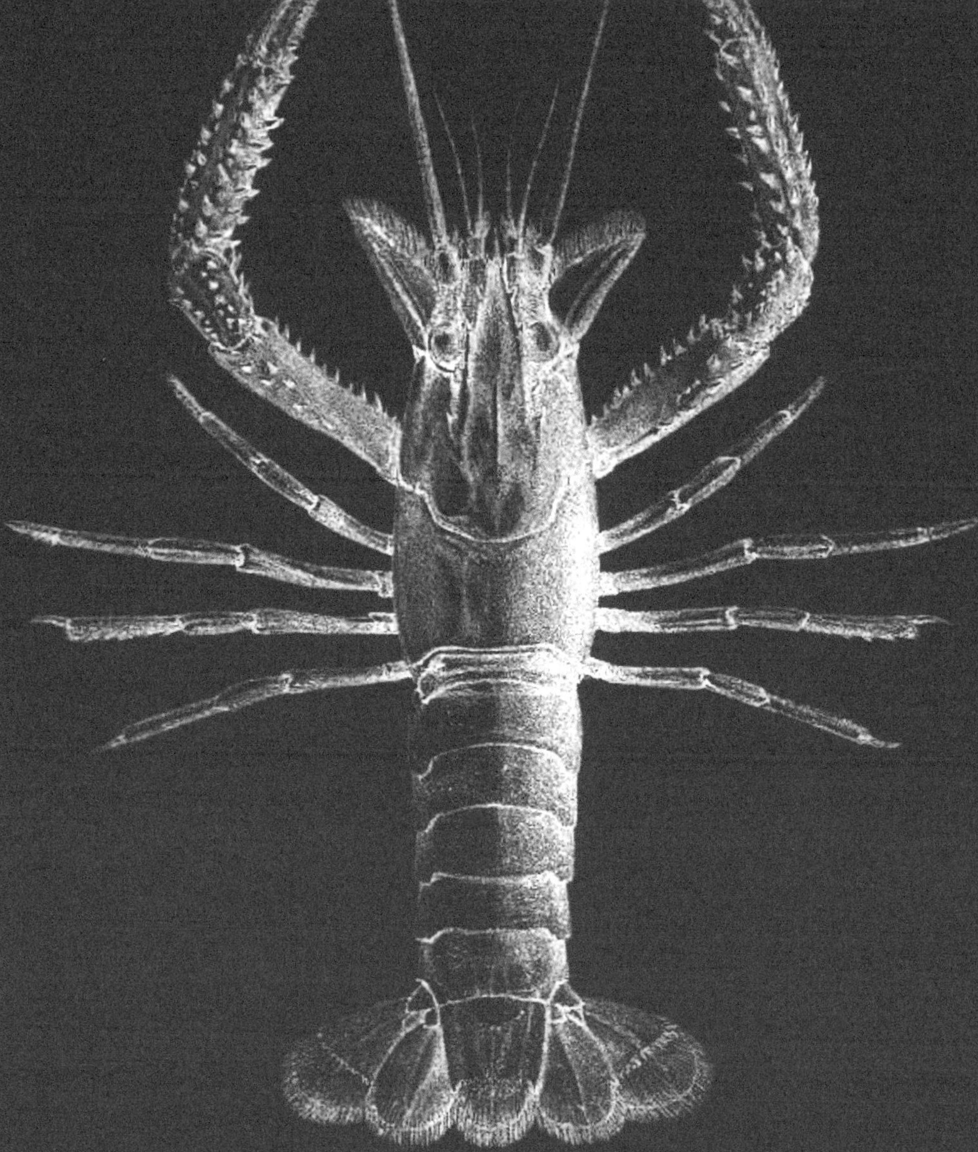